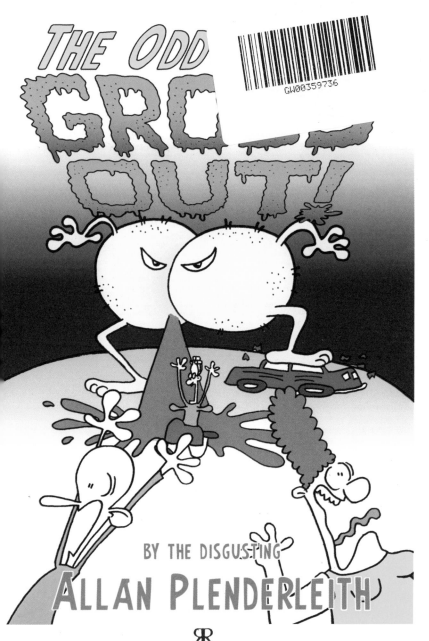

THE ODD GROW OUT!

BY THE DISGUSTING
ALLAN PLENDERLEITH

RAVETTE PUBLISHING

THE ODD SQUAD and all related characters © 2004
Created by Allan Plenderleith

First Published by
Ravette Publishing Limited 2004
Unit 3, Tristar Centre, Star Road, Partridge Green, West Sussex RH13 8RA

Printed in Malta

ISBN: 1 84161 219 7

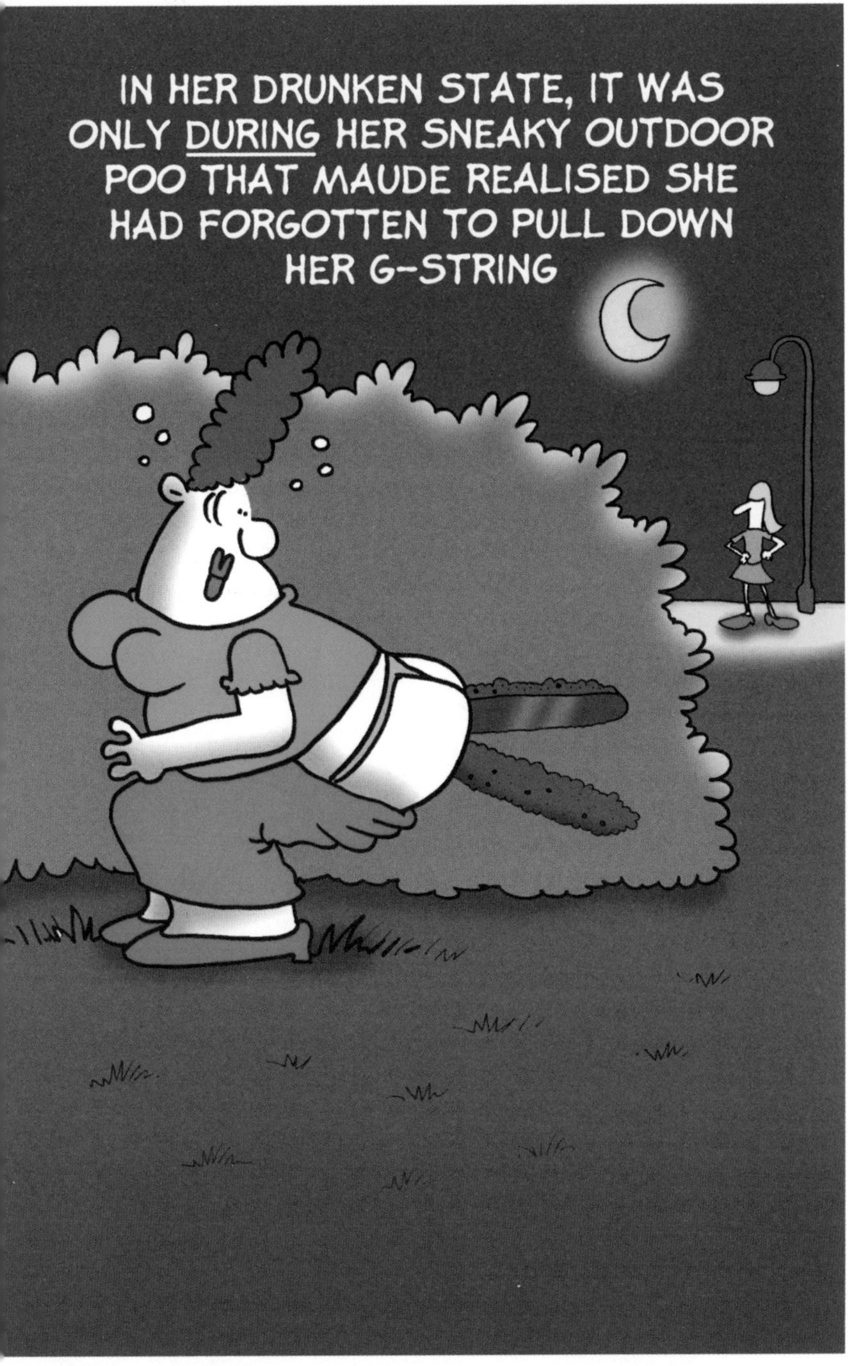
IN HER DRUNKEN STATE, IT WAS ONLY DURING HER SNEAKY OUTDOOR POO THAT MAUDE REALISED SHE HAD FORGOTTEN TO PULL DOWN HER G-STRING

HMM. THE FLOWER CERTAINLY LOOKED NICE BUT IT SMELLED TERRIBLE!

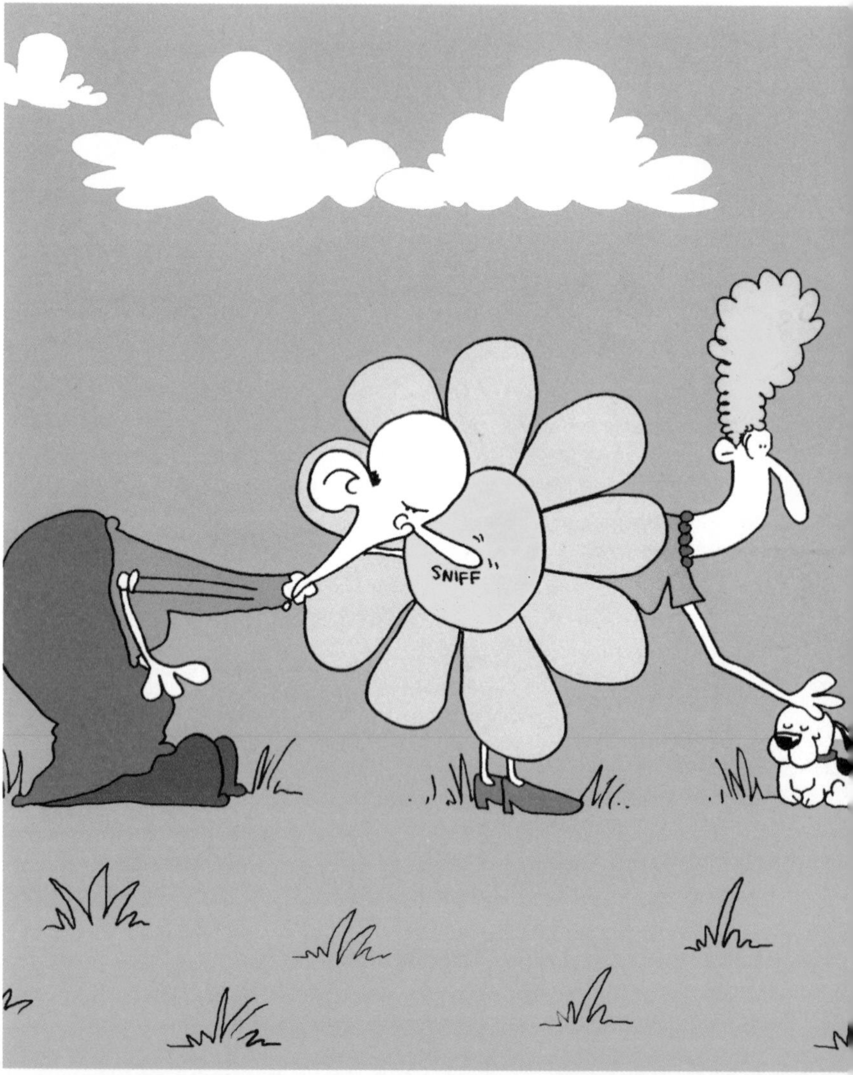
SNIFF

THE DOG HAD MADE THE MISTAKE OF LICKING LILY'S FEET AFTER SHE'D SPENT A HARD DAY SHOPPING

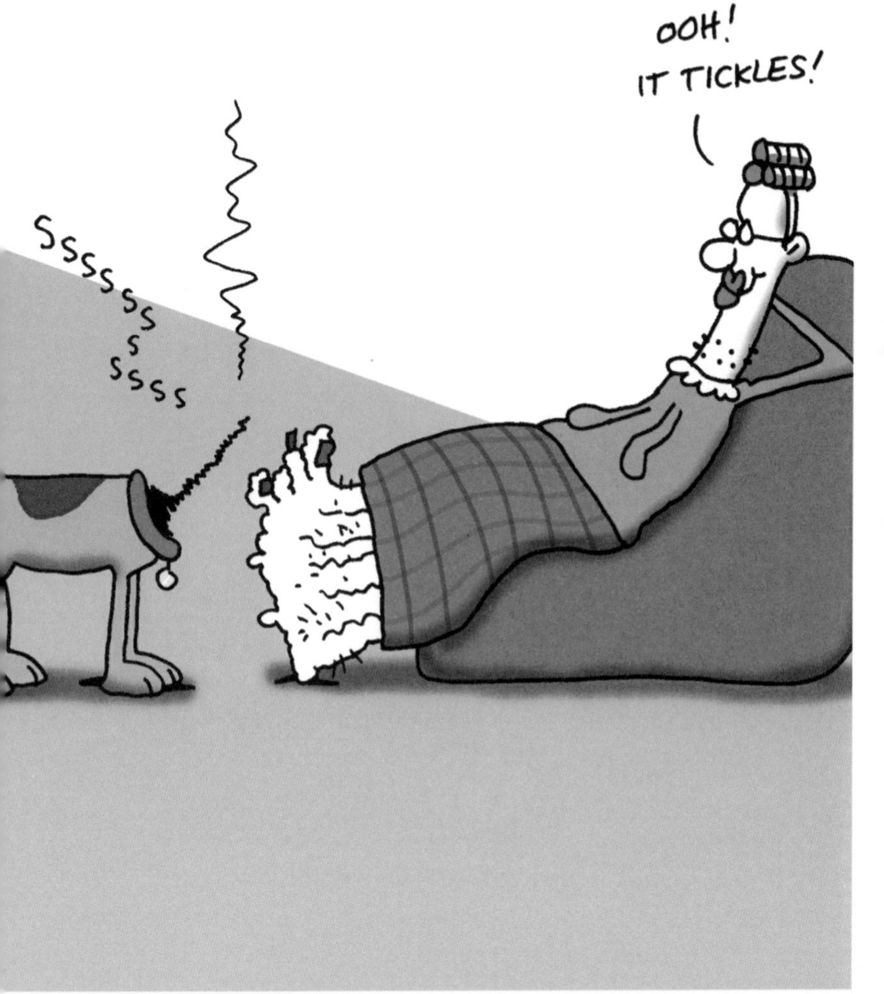
OOH! IT TICKLES!

WHAT DANDRUFF LOOKS LIKE WHEN YOU'RE BALD

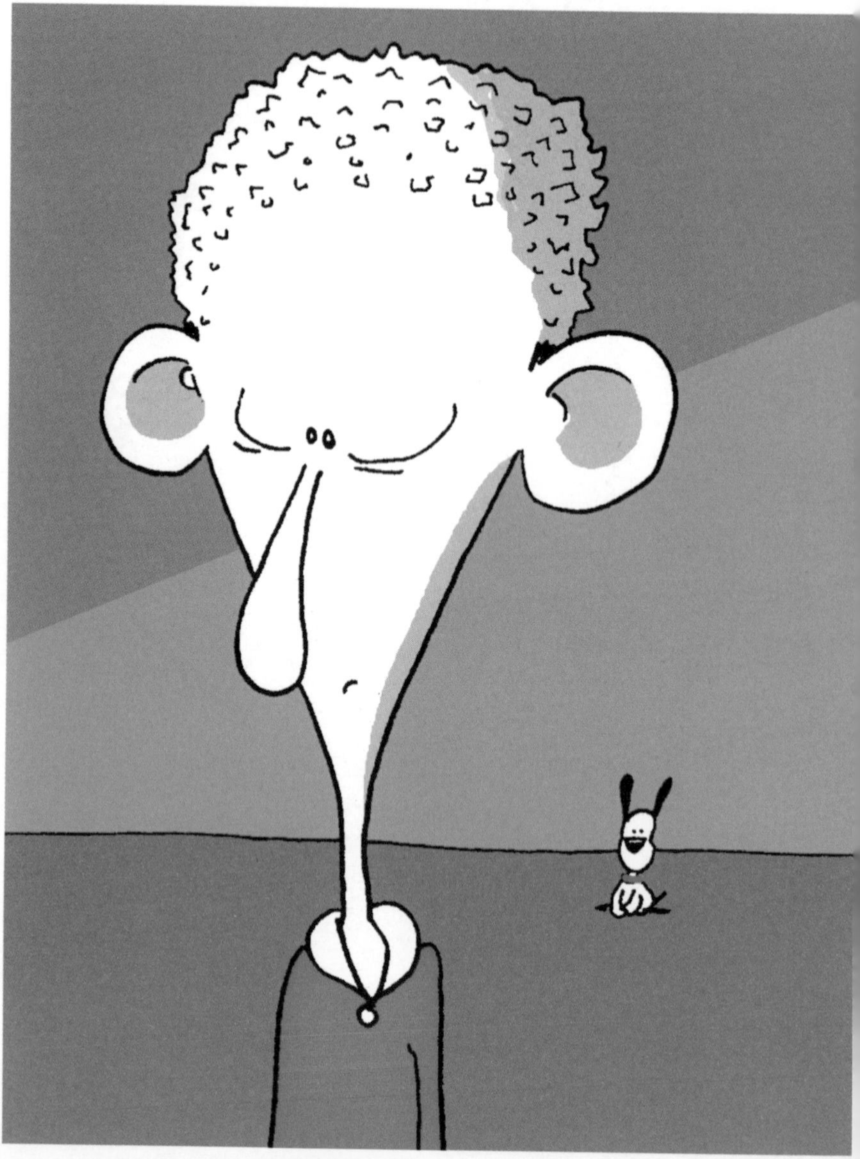

SADLY, ALF DIDN'T HAVE THE HEART TO TELL LILY THAT THE "HAMSTER" SHE HAD FOUND IN THE BATH WAS ACTUALLY THE SOAP

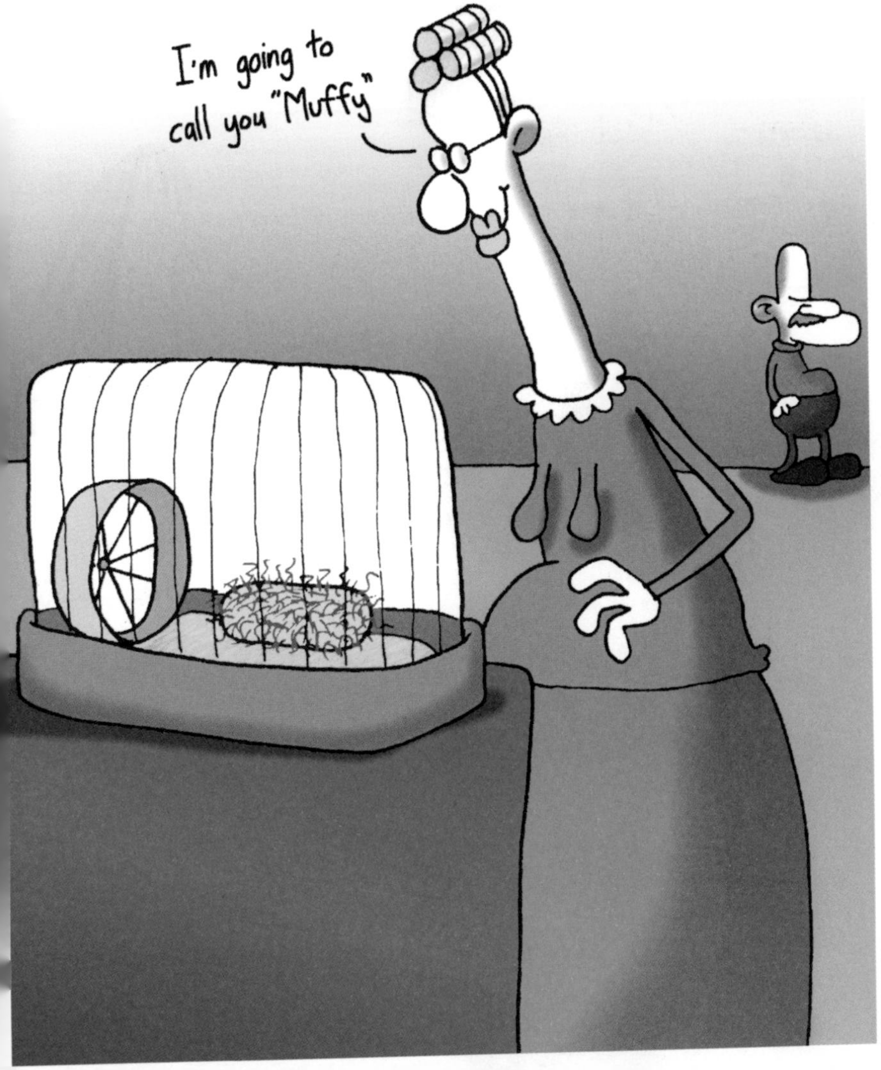
I'm going to call you "Muffy"

DUG'S DATE WITH 'BARBARA' WAS GOING GREAT, UNTIL THE TAXI LIGHTS SHONE THROUGH HER DRESS

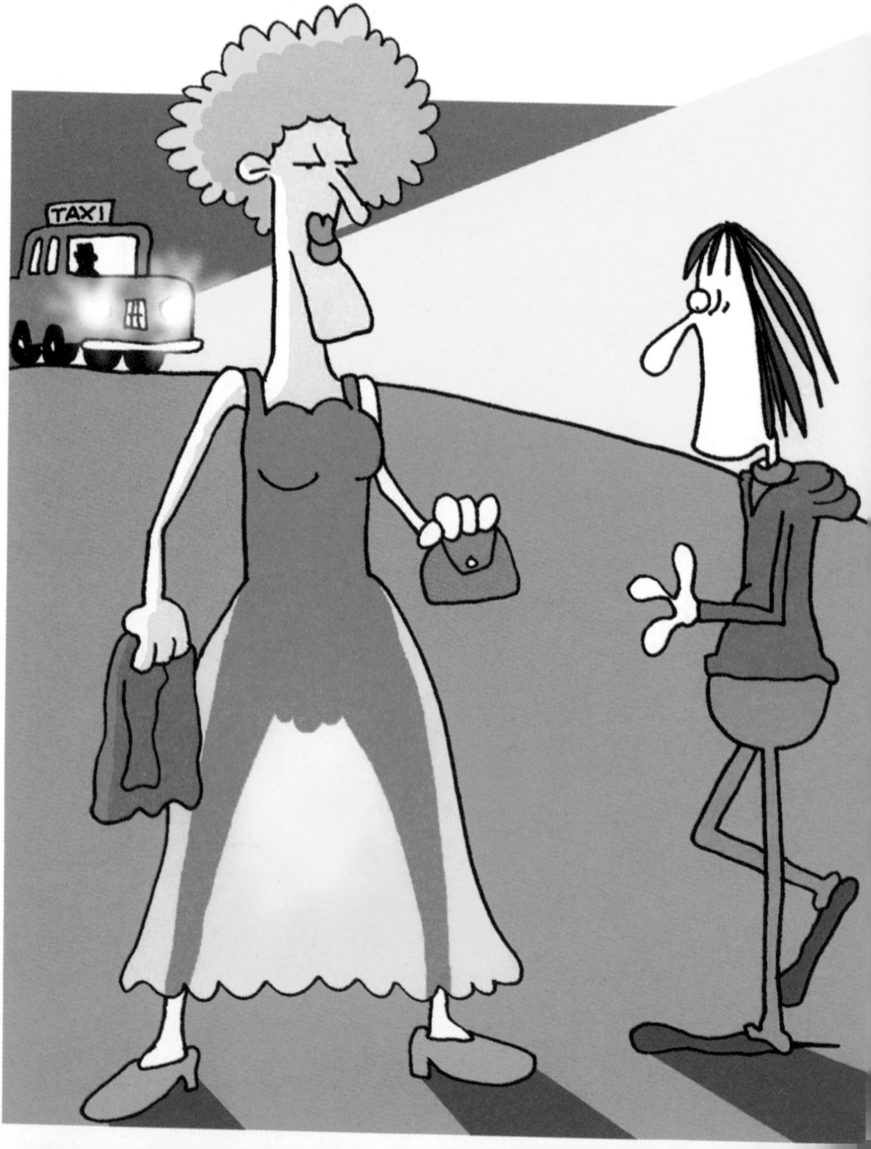
TAXI

DURING HIS LONG JOURNEY, JEFF DECIDES TO STOP ON THE HARD SHOULDER FOR A QUICK WEE

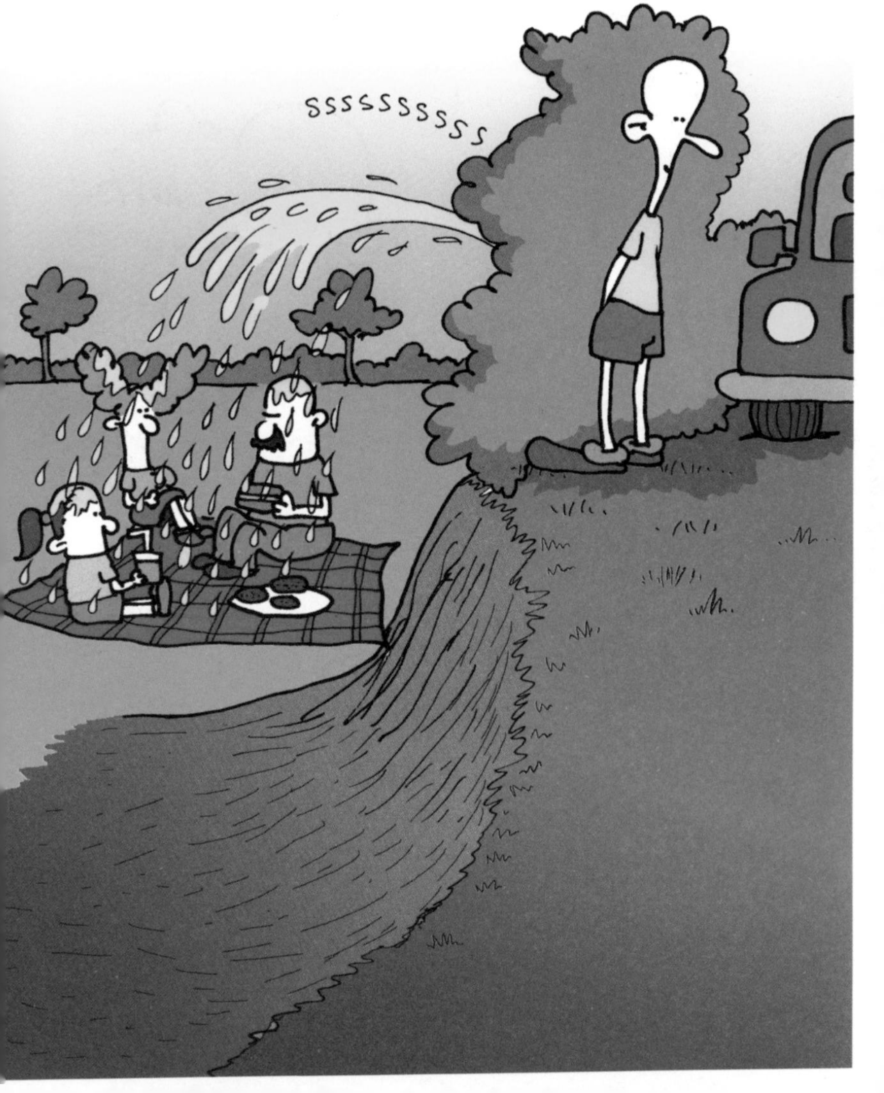
SSSSSSSSSSSS

MAUDE TRIED TO PERSUADE JEFF THAT HE WAS SPENDING TOO MUCH TIME ON HIS MOBILE

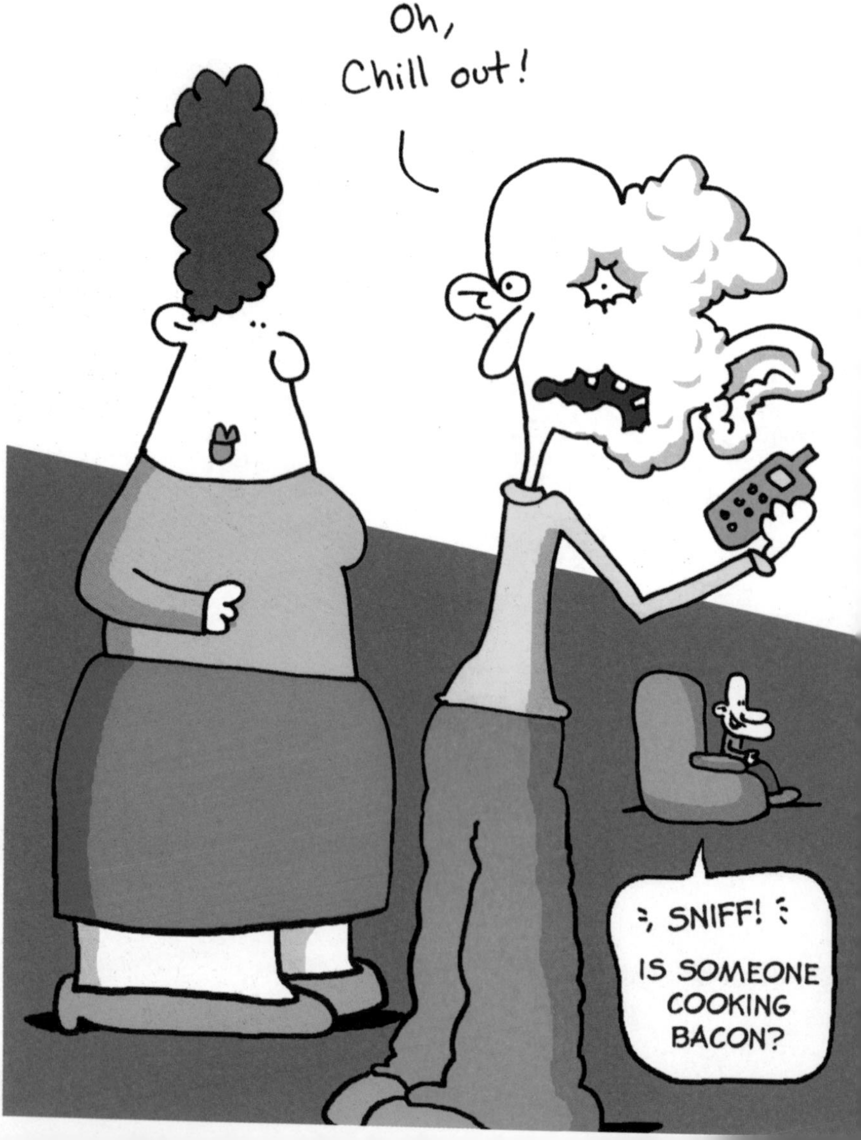

Oh, Chill out!
SNIFF!
IS SOMEONE COOKING BACON?

REALISING THAT CLEAVAGES ALWAYS GET SERVED FIRST AT A BAR, JEFF POPPED OUT HIS LITTLE PUPPIES

ONCE AGAIN, THE DOG HAD SHARPENED THE STRINGS ON JEFF'S GUITAR

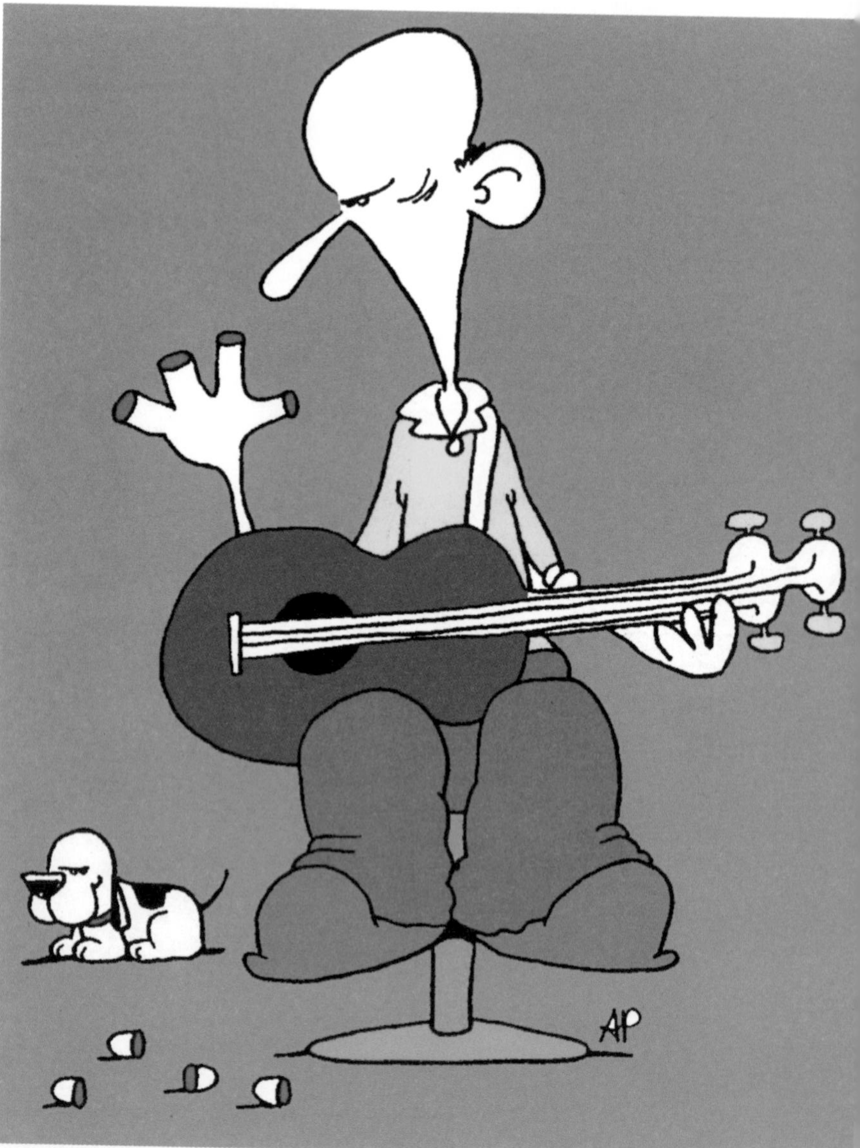
AP

SUDDENLY, MAUDE REGRETTED WEARING RASPBERRY LIP GLOSS ON A SUMMER'S DAY

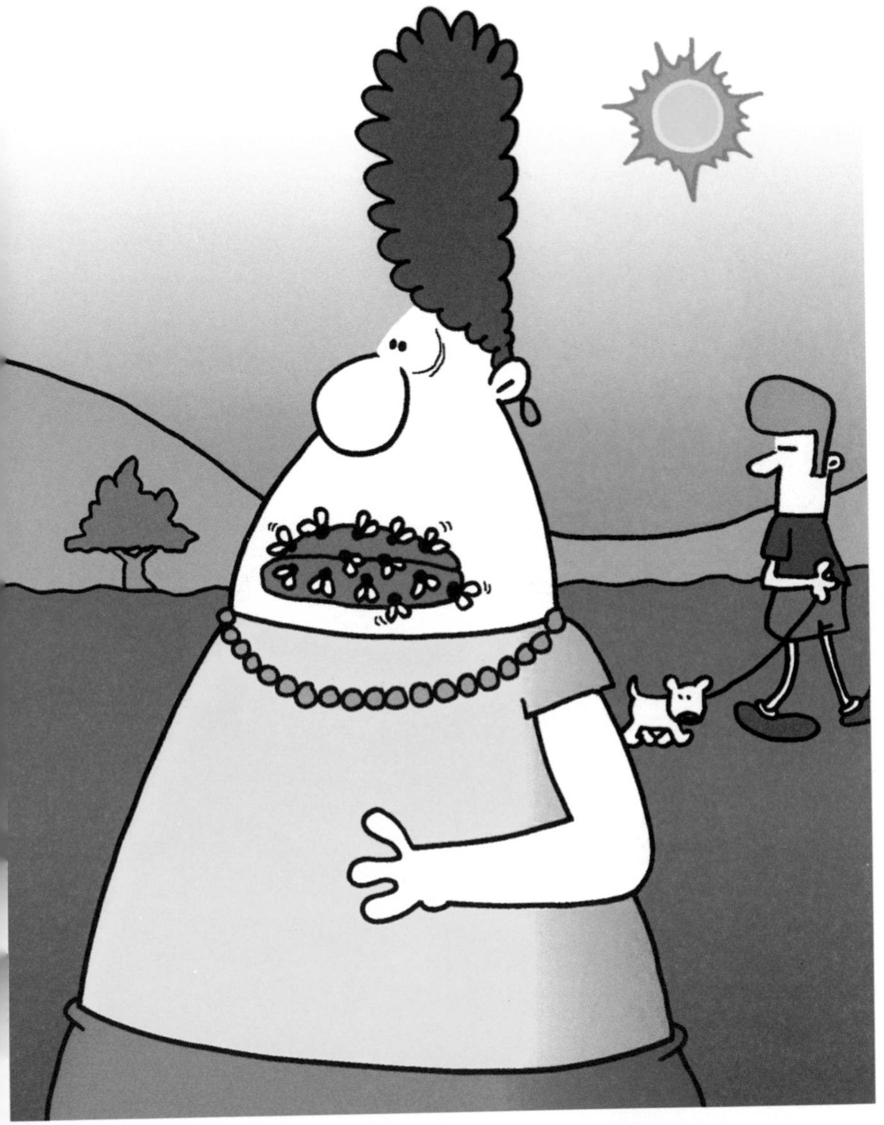

ANNOYINGLY, THE CAT WAS ALWAYS TOO FORCEFUL WHEN COVERING UP ITS POO IN THE KITTY LITTER

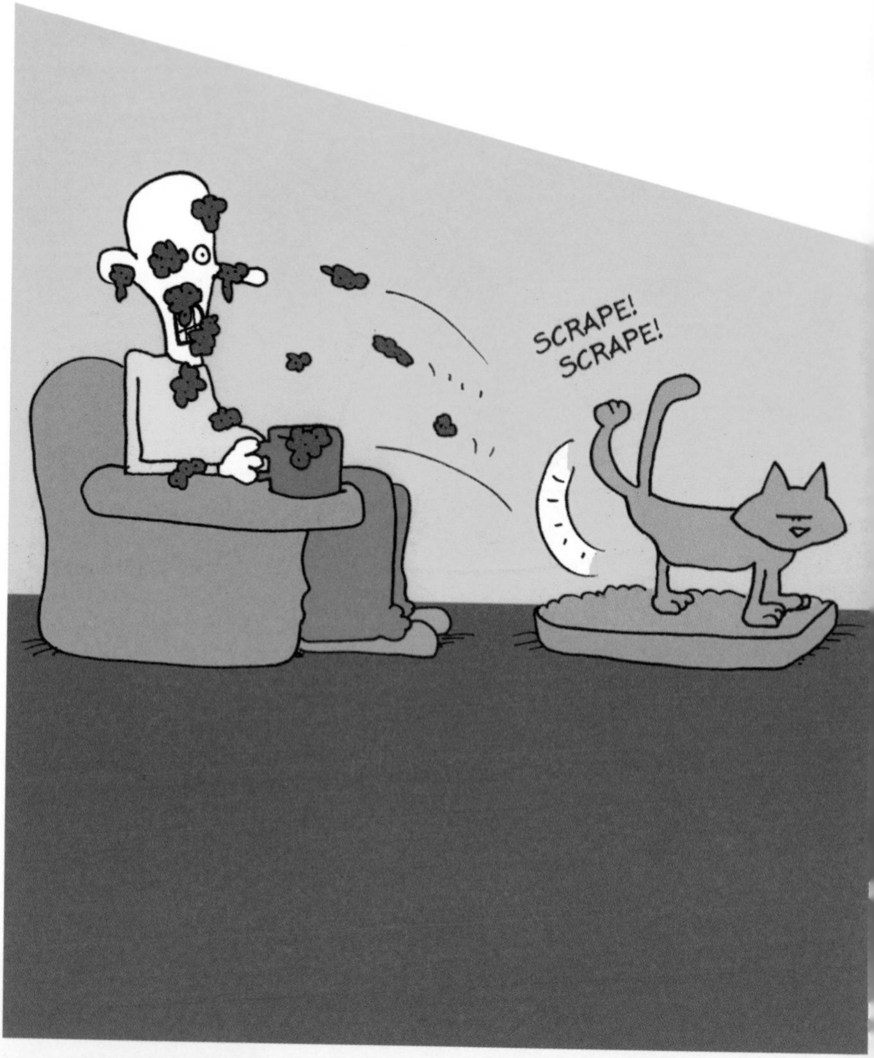
SCRAPE!
SCRAPE!

HAVING RUN OUT OF MARZIPAN, LILY OPTS FOR PLAN B

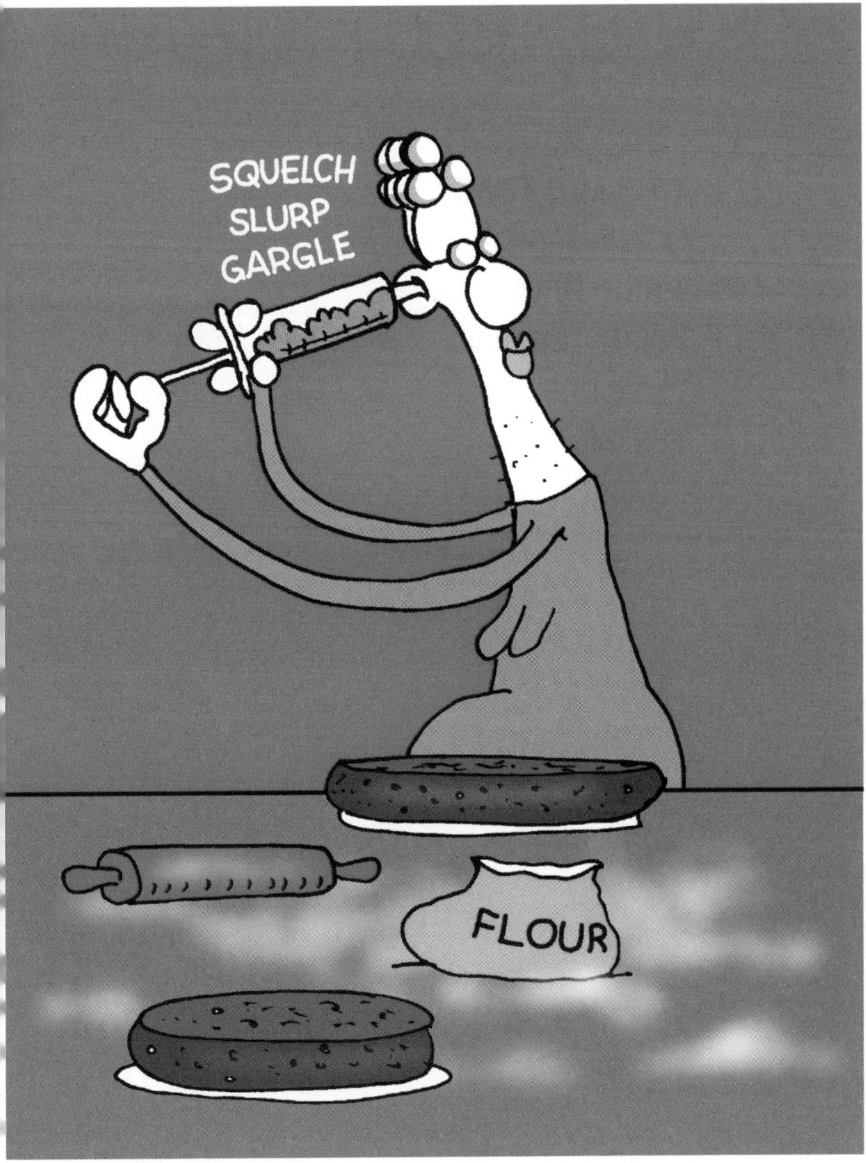
SQUELCH
SLURP
GARGLE
FLOUR

The HORRIBLE TRUTH ABOUT MEN!
1
TO SAVE TIME IN THE MORNING WHILE BRUSHING THEIR TEETH, THEY PEE INTO THE SINK
SPLASH
GARGLE
2
THEY CUP THEIR FARTS AND SMELL THEM
Oh, good one.

3 THEY NEVER WASH THEIR HANDS AFTER GOING TO THE TOILET

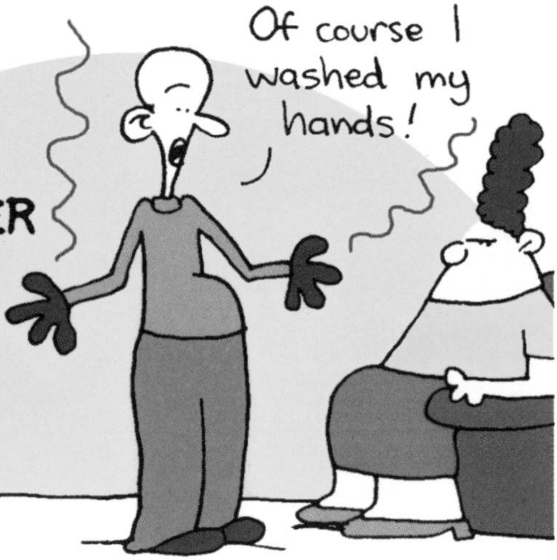
Of course I washed my hands!

4 AS SOON AS THEY'RE ALONE THEY'LL START PLAYING WITH THEIR WILLIES.

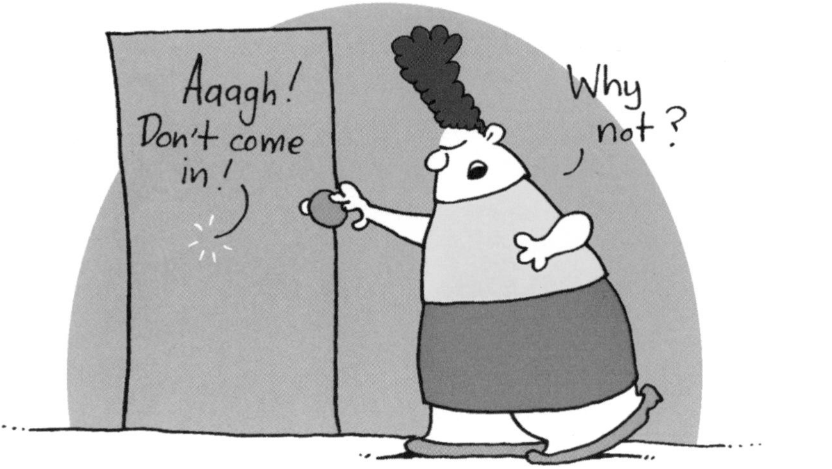
Aaagh! Don't come in!
Why not?

OVER THE YEARS, JEFF HAD LEARNED TO UNDERSTAND EXACTLY WHAT THE DOG WAS THINKING

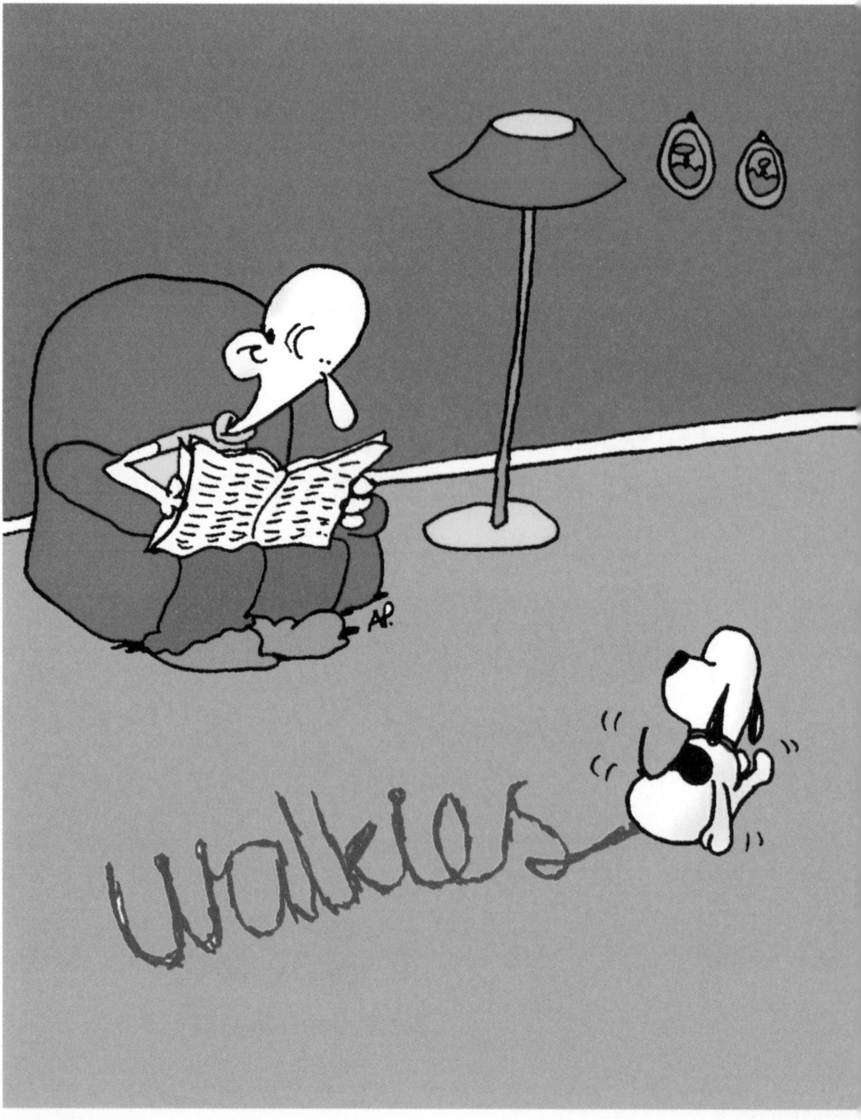
walkies

JEFF WAS JUST CLEANING HIS EAR WITH A PENCIL WHEN MAUDE BUMPED HIS ELBOW WITH THE DOOR

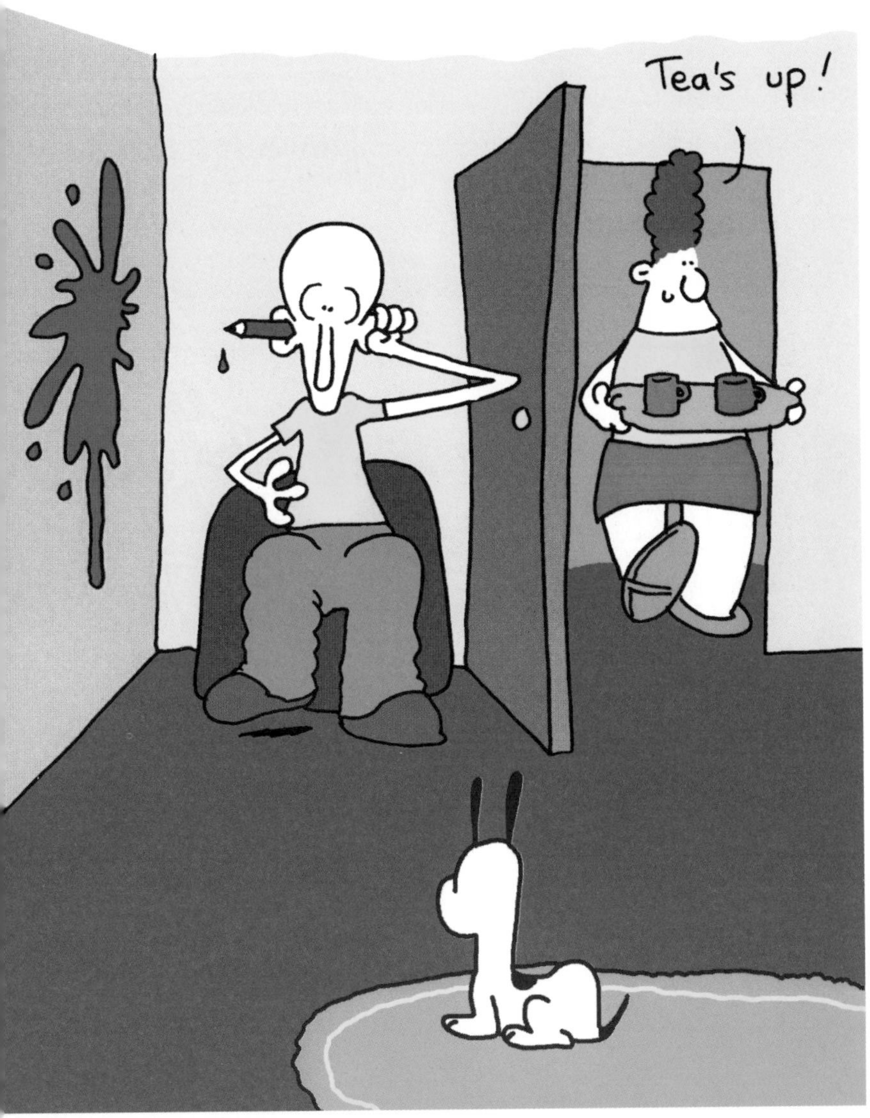
Tea's up!

AS THEY GROW OLDER, MEN'S HAIR BEGINS GROWING RAPIDLY IN THE STRANGEST PLACES

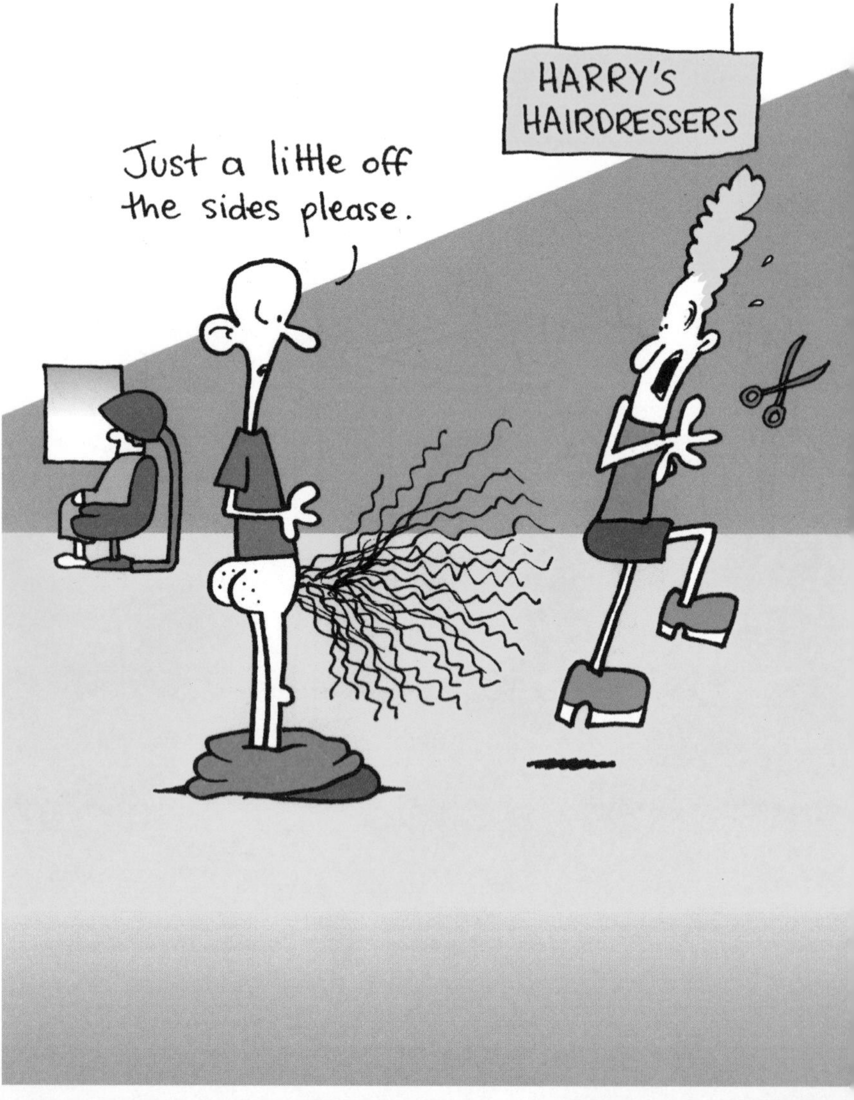
HARRY'S HAIRDRESSERS
Just a little off the sides please.

DUG WAS PLEASANTLY SURPRISED WHEN, DURING THEIR LOVE MAKING, BARBARA STARTED TICKLING HIS BUM

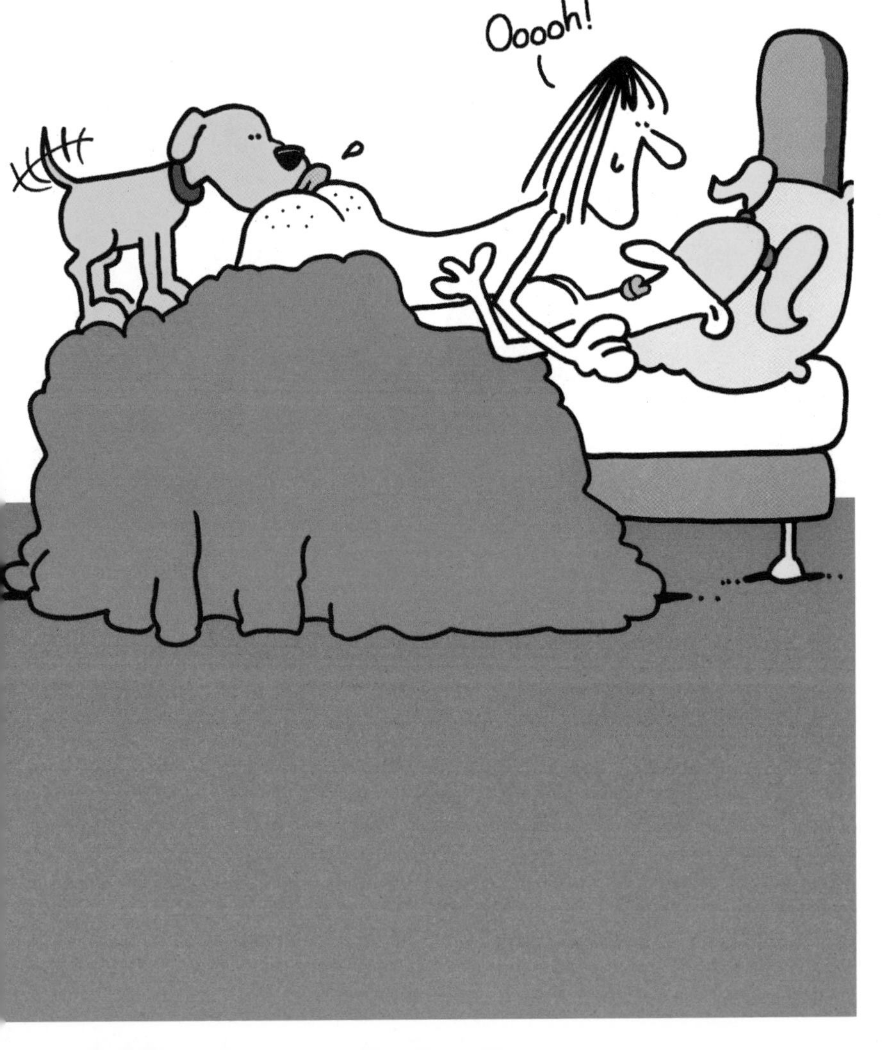
Ooooh!

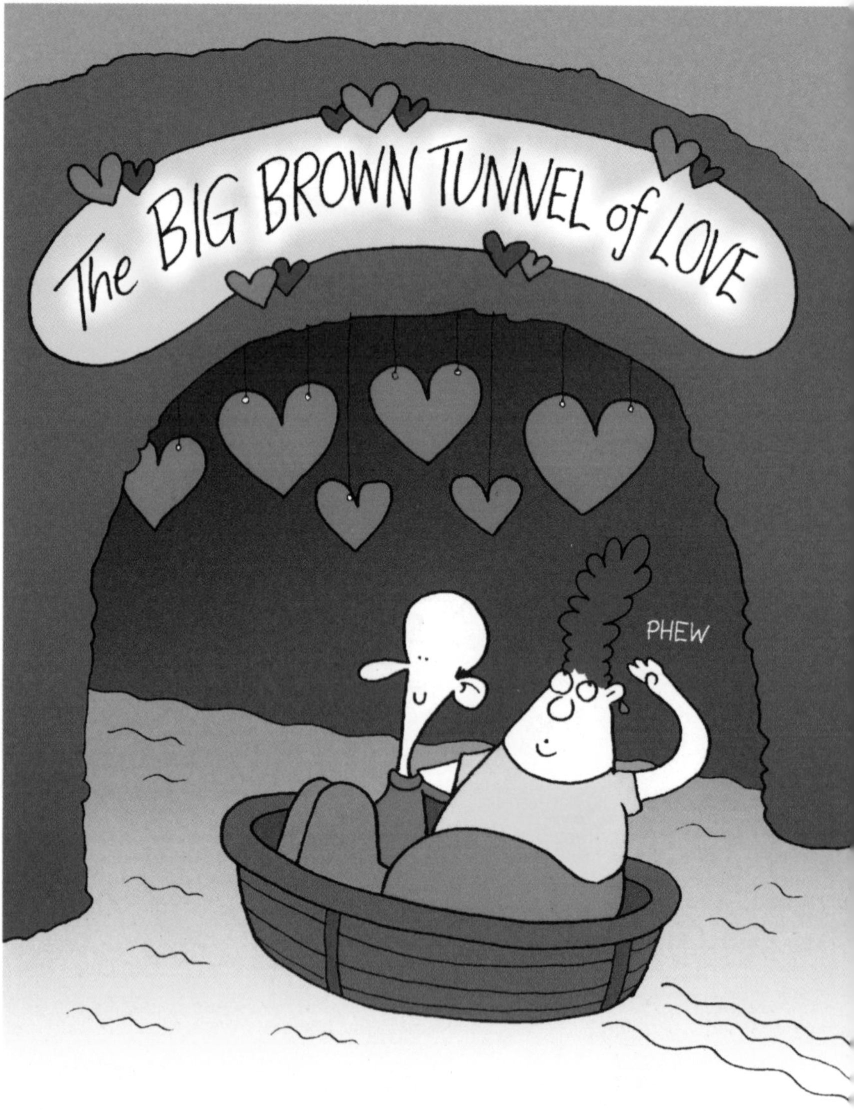
The BIG BROWN TUNNEL of LOVE
PHEW

WHEN JEFF SAID HE WANTED TO "GO UP THE BIG BROWN TUNNEL OF LOVE" SHE WAS RELIEVED TO DISCOVER HE WASN'T BEING METAPHORICAL

DUG MAKES THE MISTAKE OF GOING FOR A PEE IMMEDIATELY AFTER SEX

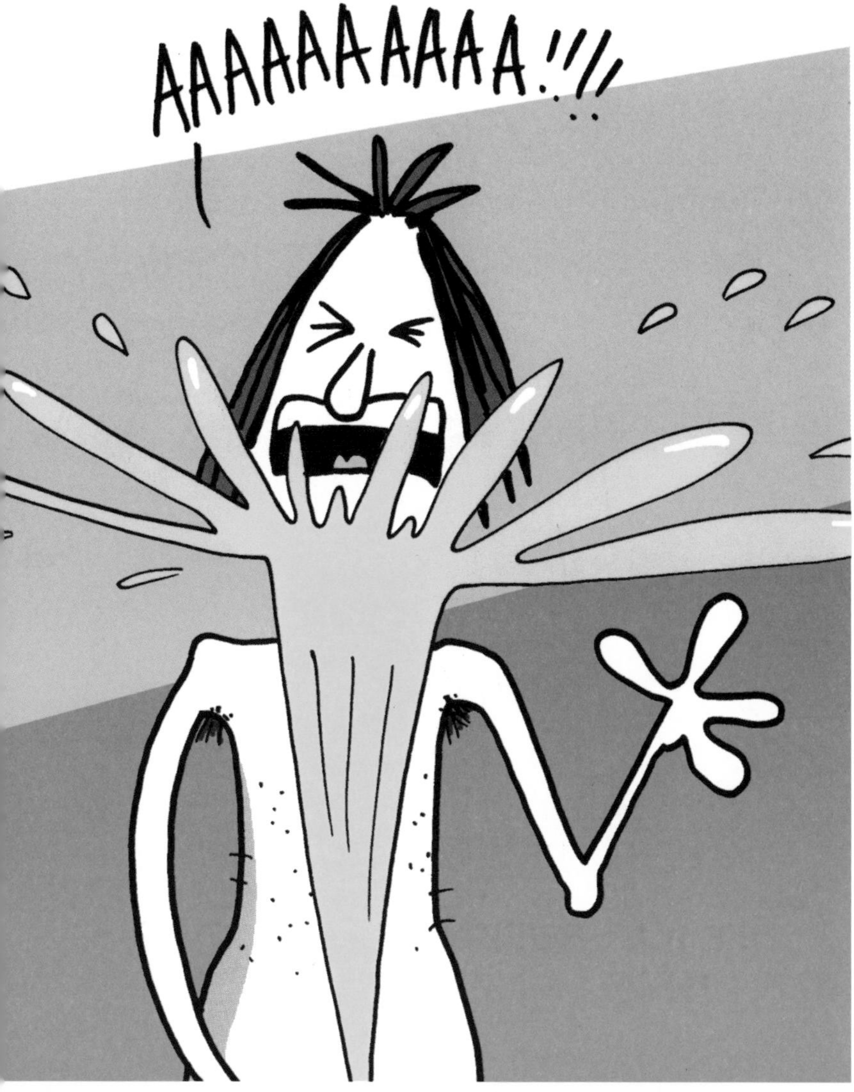
AAAAAAAAAA!!!

A WET FART IS BAD AT ANY TIME, BUT WORSE WHEN YOU'RE WEARING SHORTS

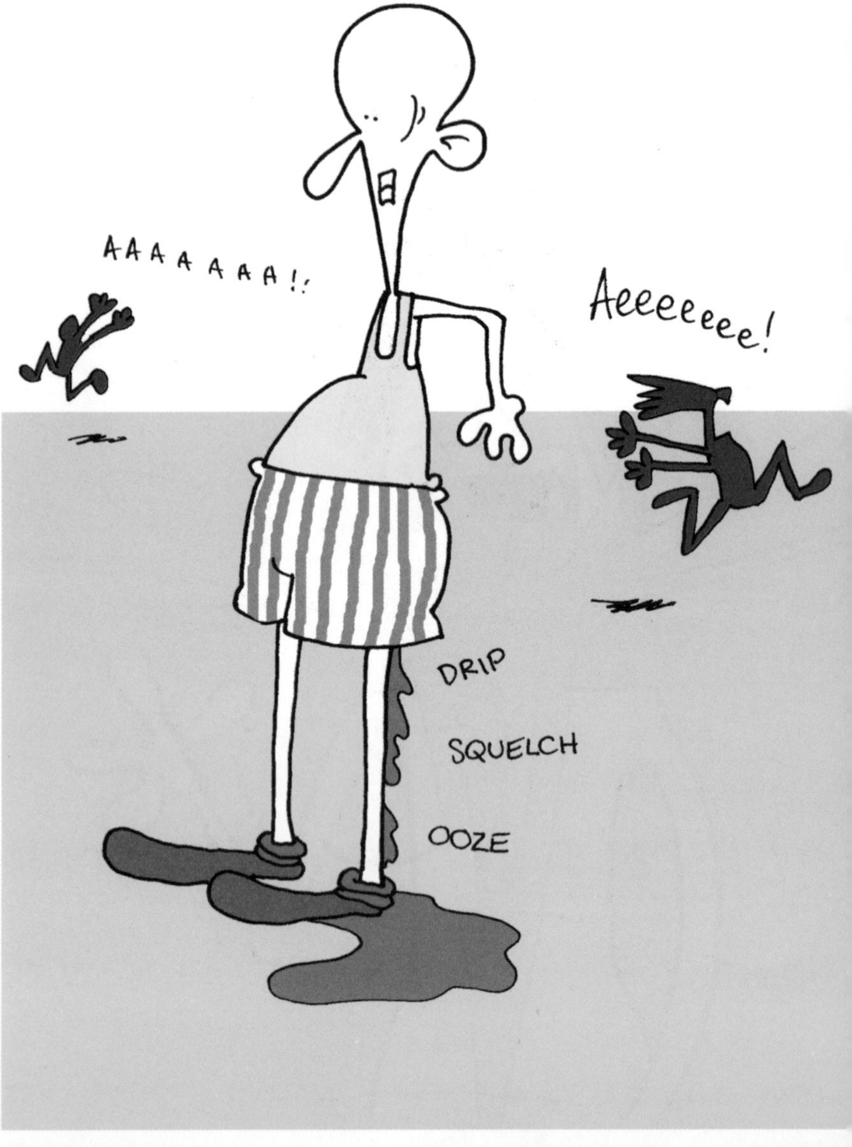
AAAAAAAA!!
Aeeeeeeee!
DRIP
SQUELCH
OOZE

JEFF HAD A FEELING THE
KEBAB WASN'T ENTIRELY
MADE FROM LAMB

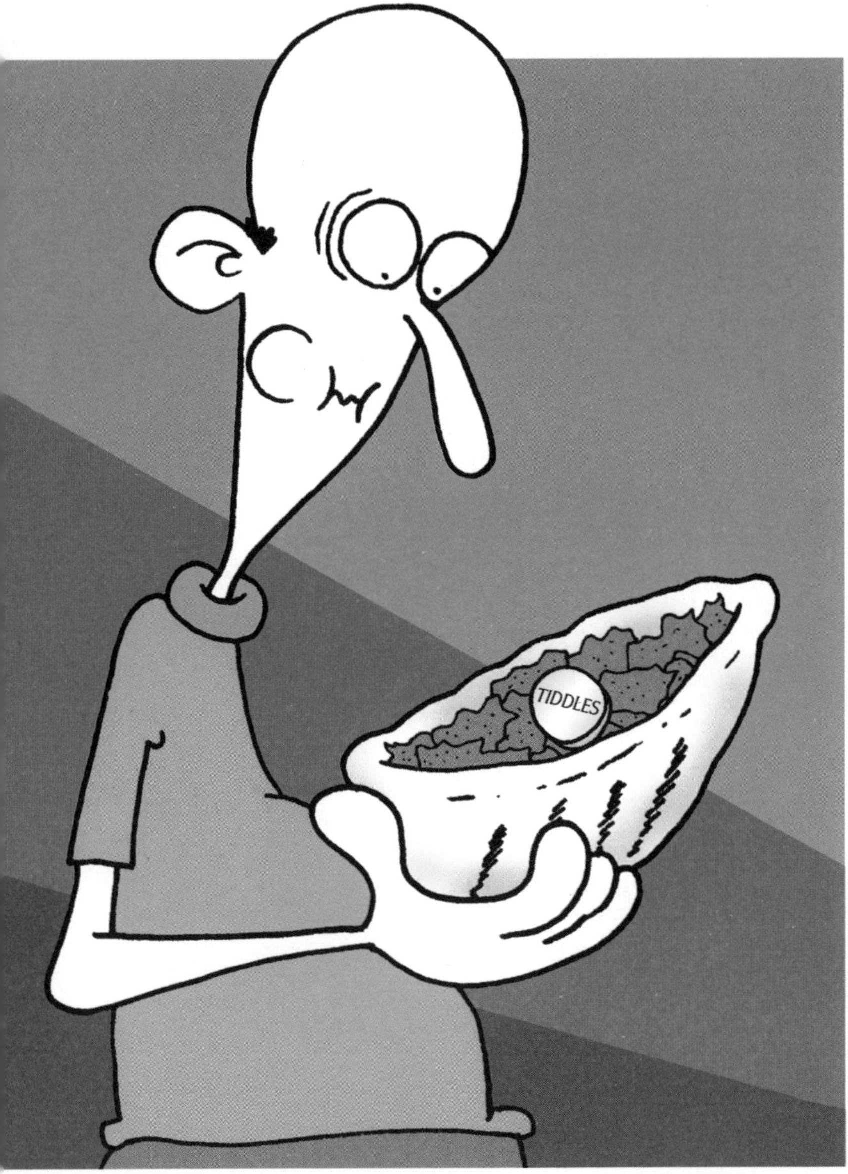
TIDDLES

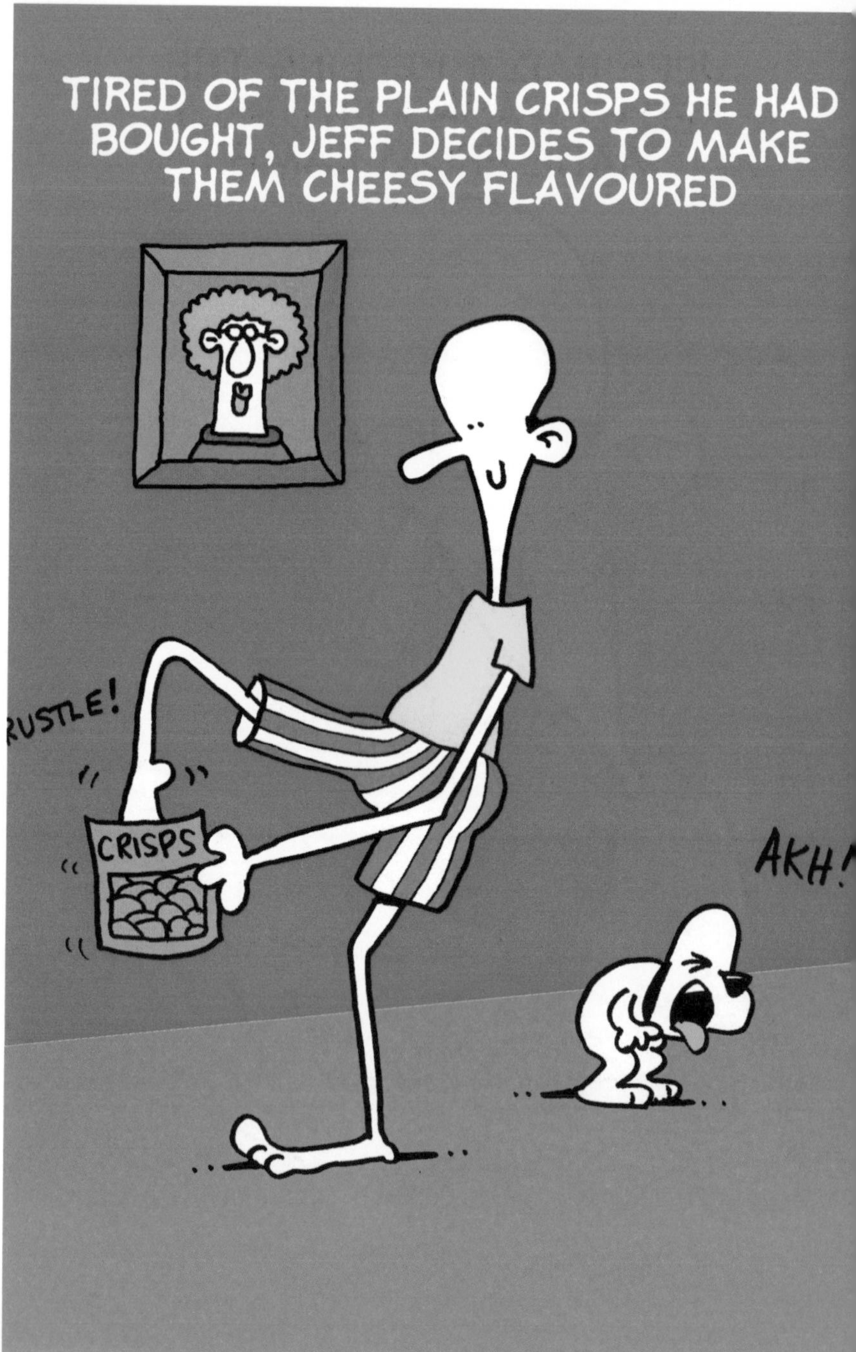
TIRED OF THE PLAIN CRISPS HE HAD BOUGHT, JEFF DECIDES TO MAKE THEM CHEESY FLAVOURED
RUSTLE!
CRISPS
AKH!

JEFF'S ATTEMPTS TO UNBLOCK HIS EARS ON THE PLANE HAD UNEXPECTED RESULTS

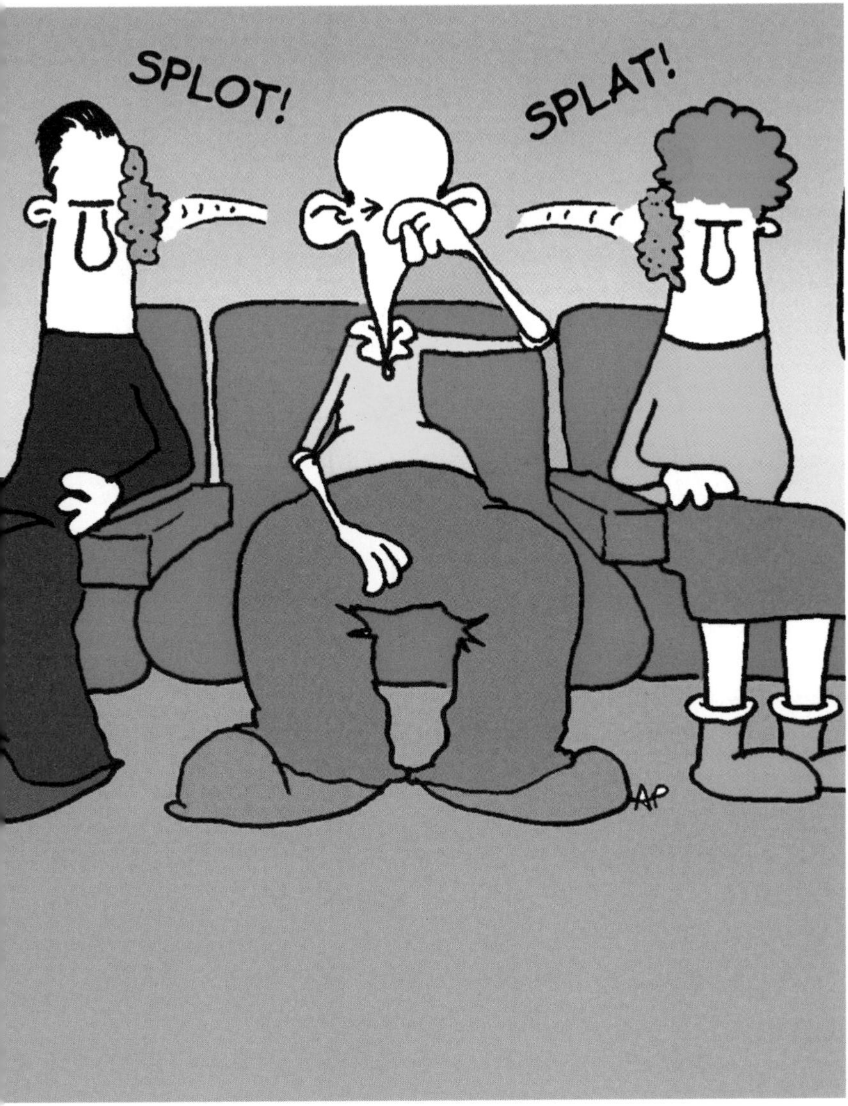
SPLOT!
SPLAT!
AP

WHY IT'S IMPORTANT TO CONCENTRATE WHEN OPERATING A CHAINSAW

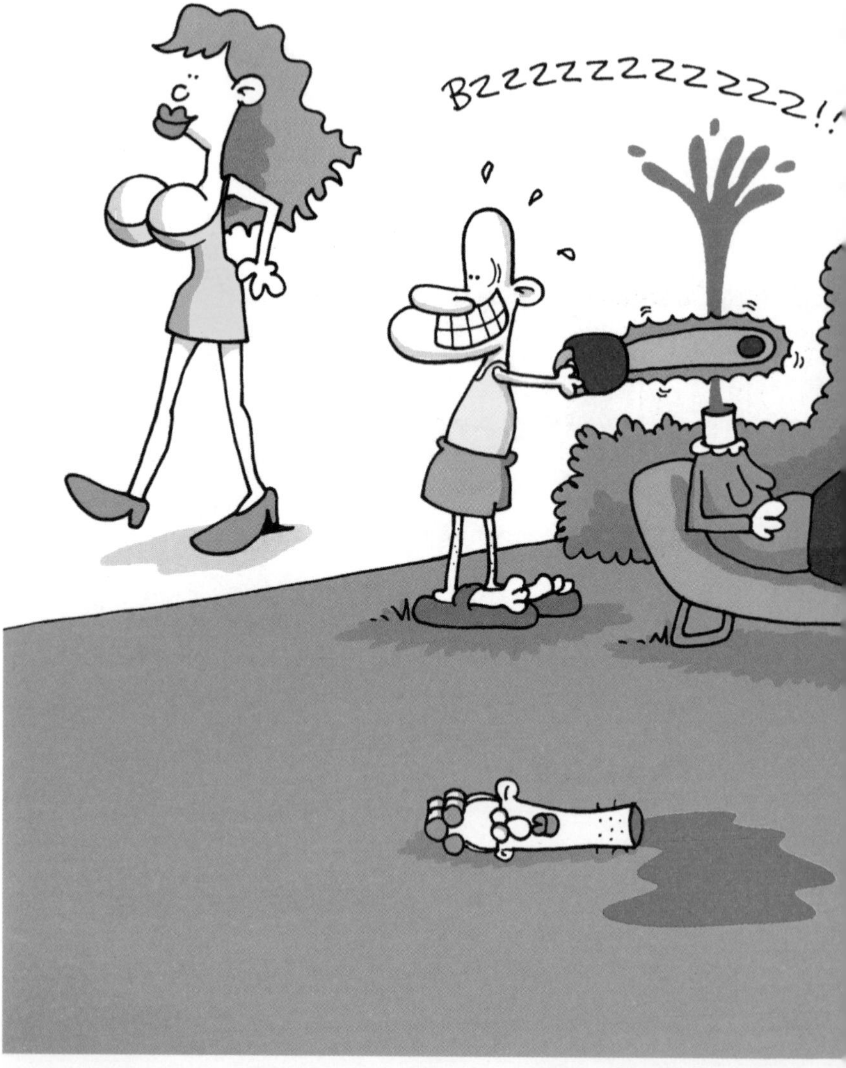
BZZZZZZZZZZZZZZ!!

UNABLE TO MAKE HER MIND UP
AT THE CARPET STORE,
LILY ASKED THE ASSISTANT
FOR A SAMPLE

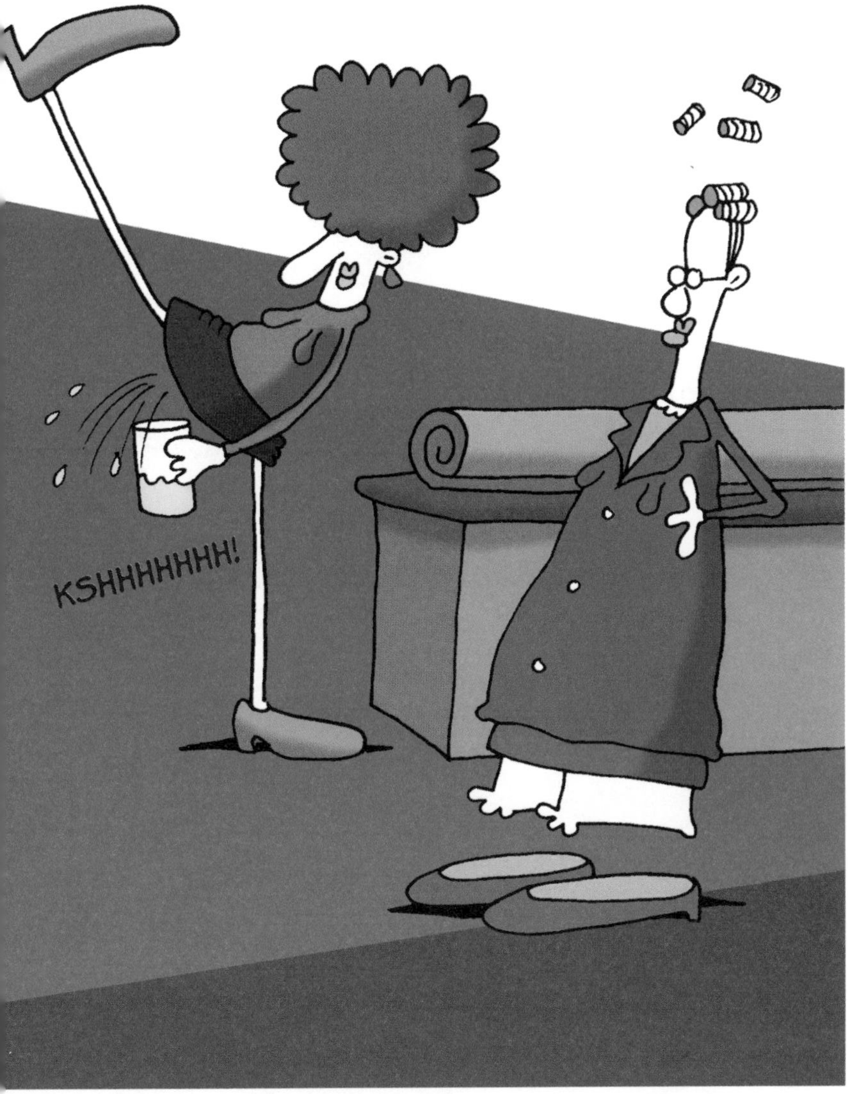
KSHHHHHHH!

UNBEKNOWN TO LILY, THE HAMSTER HAD DECIDED THE COOKIES SHE WAS MAKING SHOULD BE CHOCOLATE CHIP

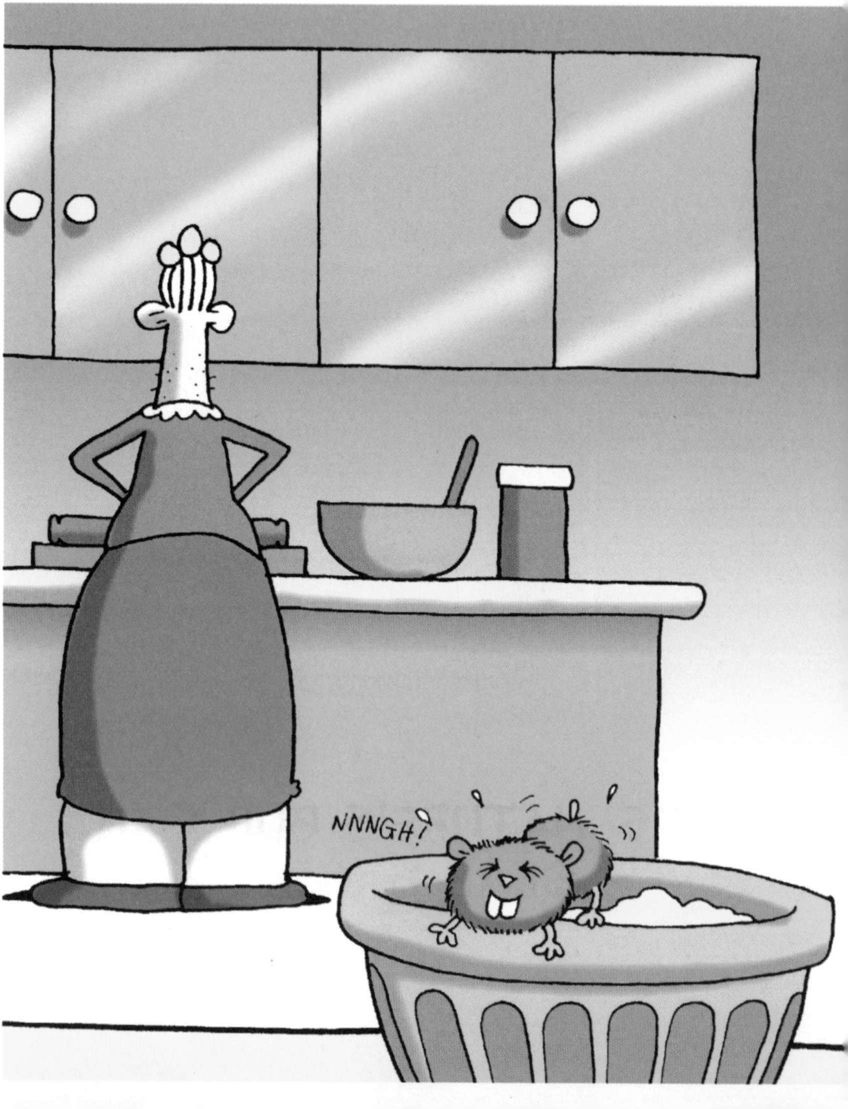
NNNGH!

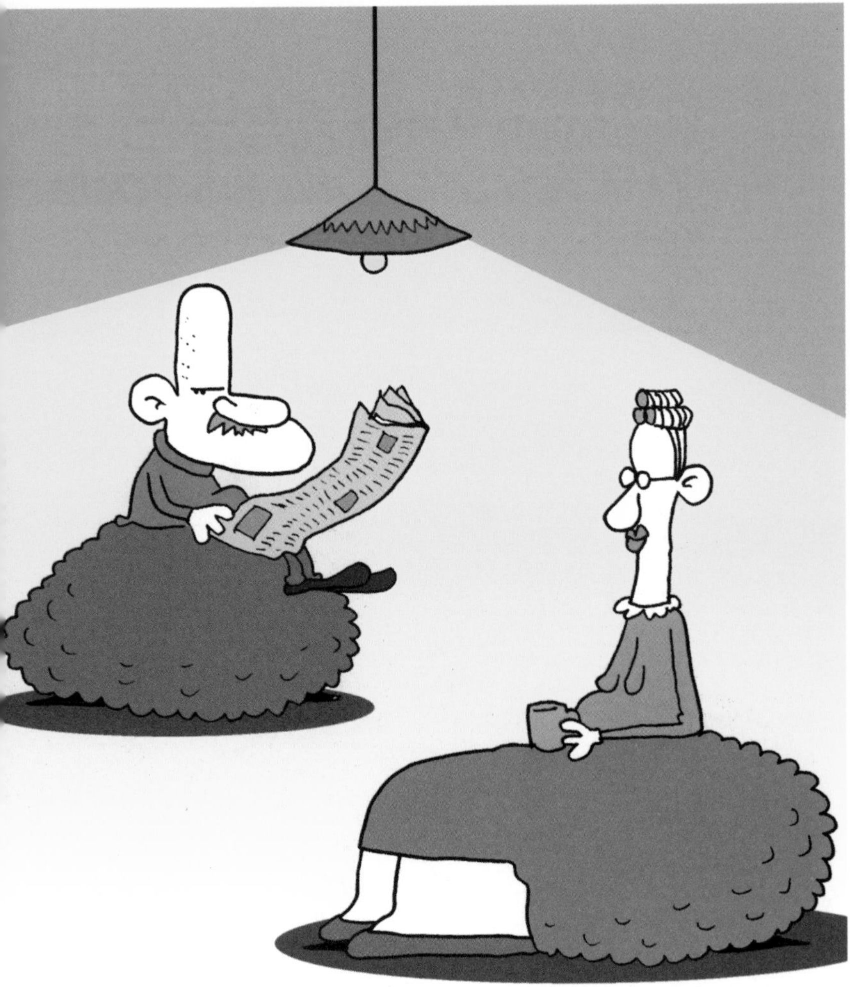

PILES: NATURE'S BUILT-IN
BEAN BAGS

DUG FINALLY FIGURES OUT
A WAY TO STOP HIS
FLATMATES STEALING HIS FOOD

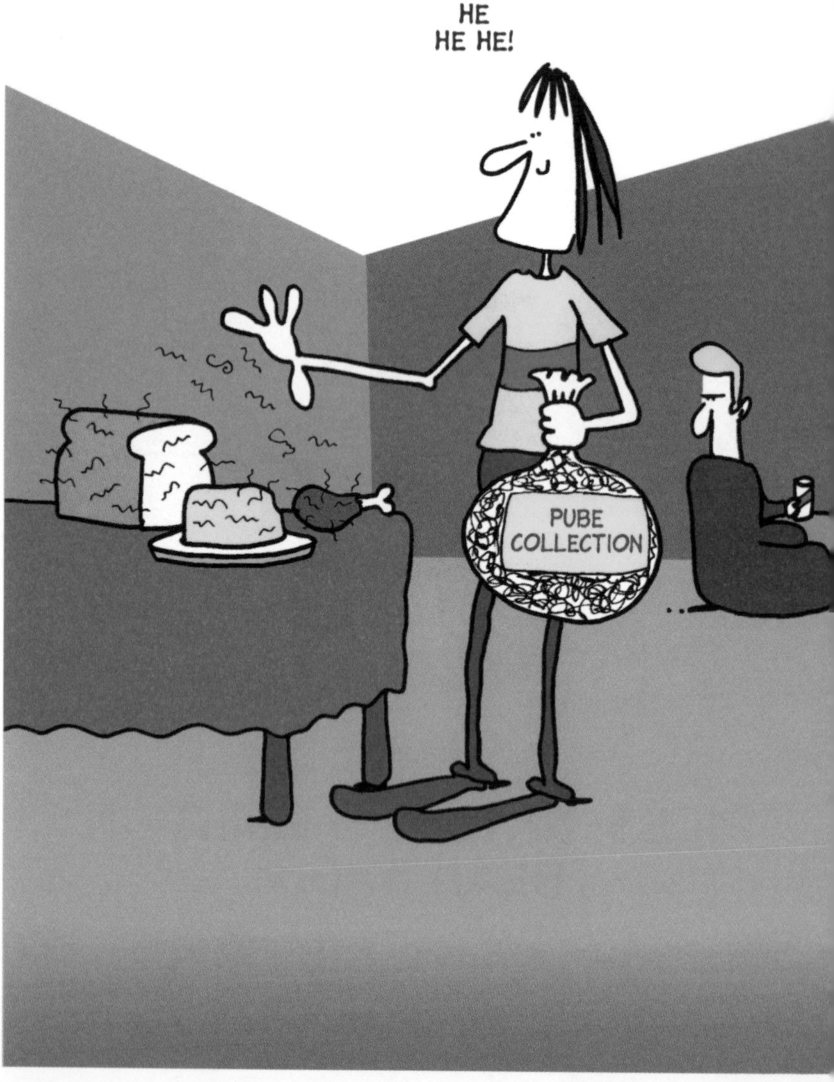
HE
HE HE!
PUBE
COLLECTION

EVEN THOUGH SHE WAS DRUNK, MAUDE ALWAYS MANAGED TO TAKE HER FACE OFF

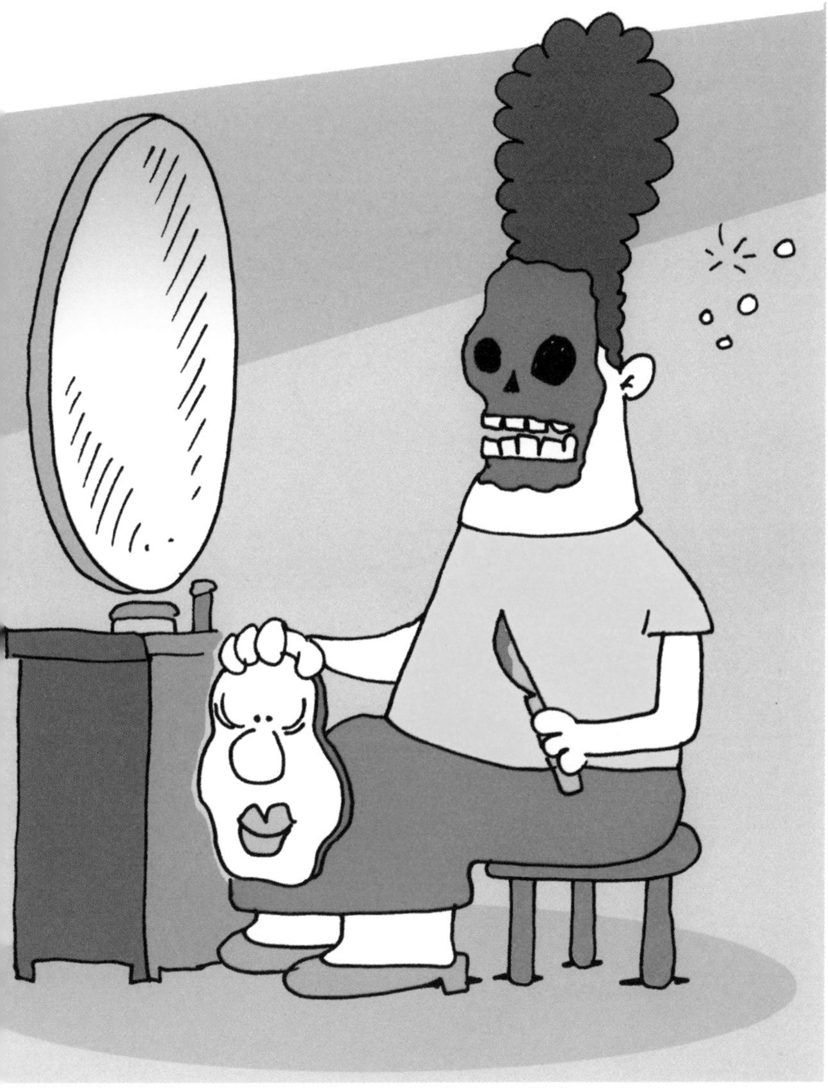

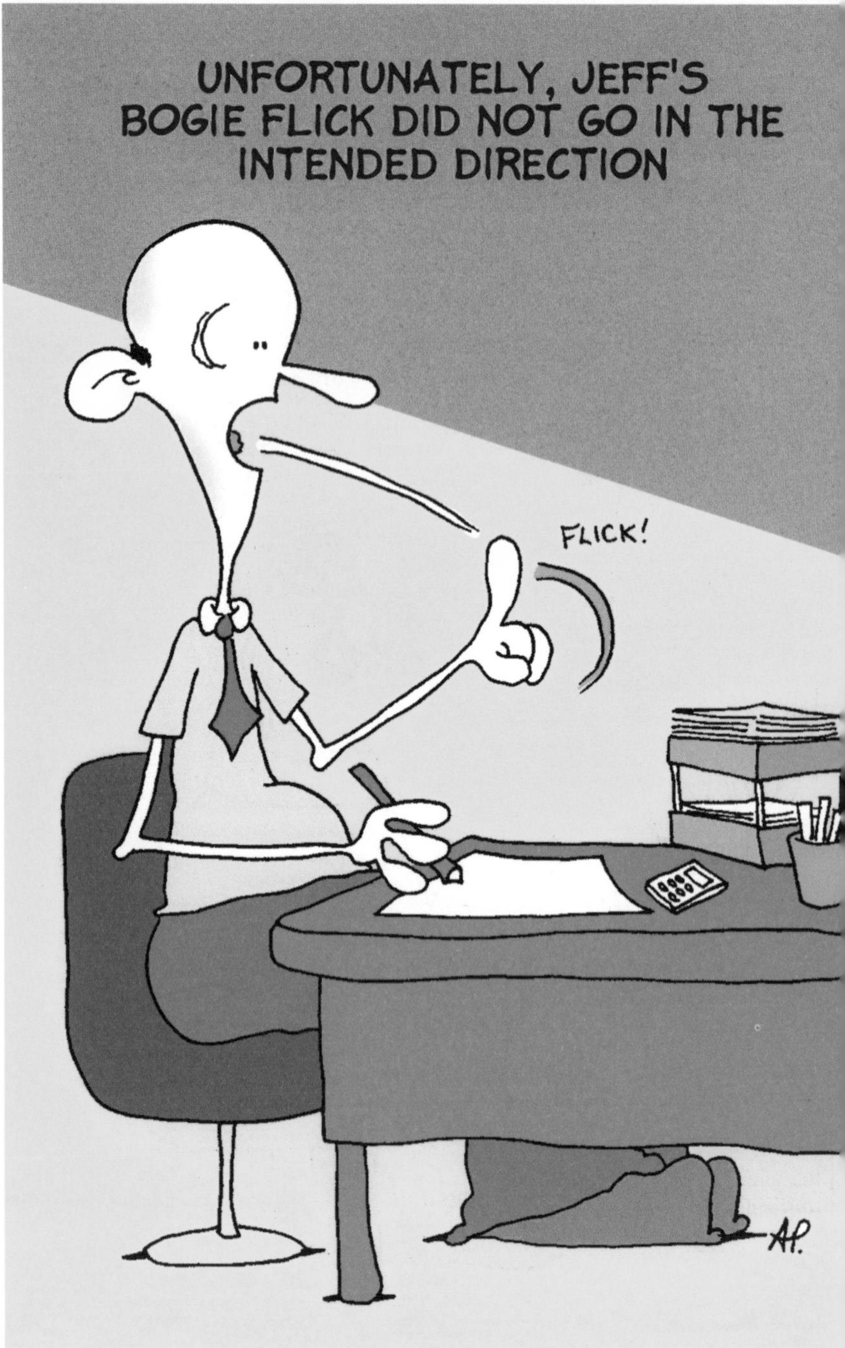
UNFORTUNATELY, JEFF'S BOGIE FLICK DID NOT GO IN THE INTENDED DIRECTION
FLICK!
AP.

MAUDE ONLY REALISED HER BUM WASN'T CLEAN WHEN 'BERTY BIG CHIN' CAME UP FOR AIR

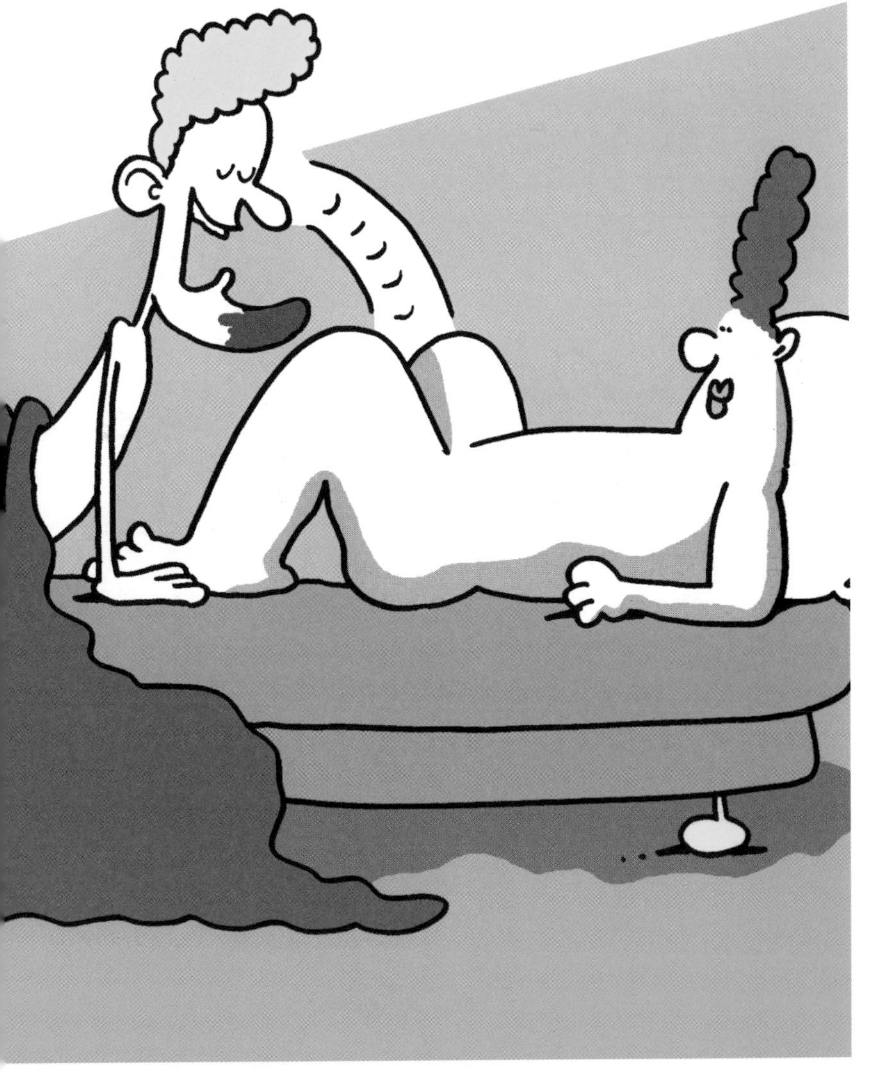

JEFF GIGGLED – HE JUST REMEMBERED THE BIZARRE DREAM HE'D HAD ABOUT KILLING A FAT GROWLING MONSTER BY DUMPING IN ITS MOUTH

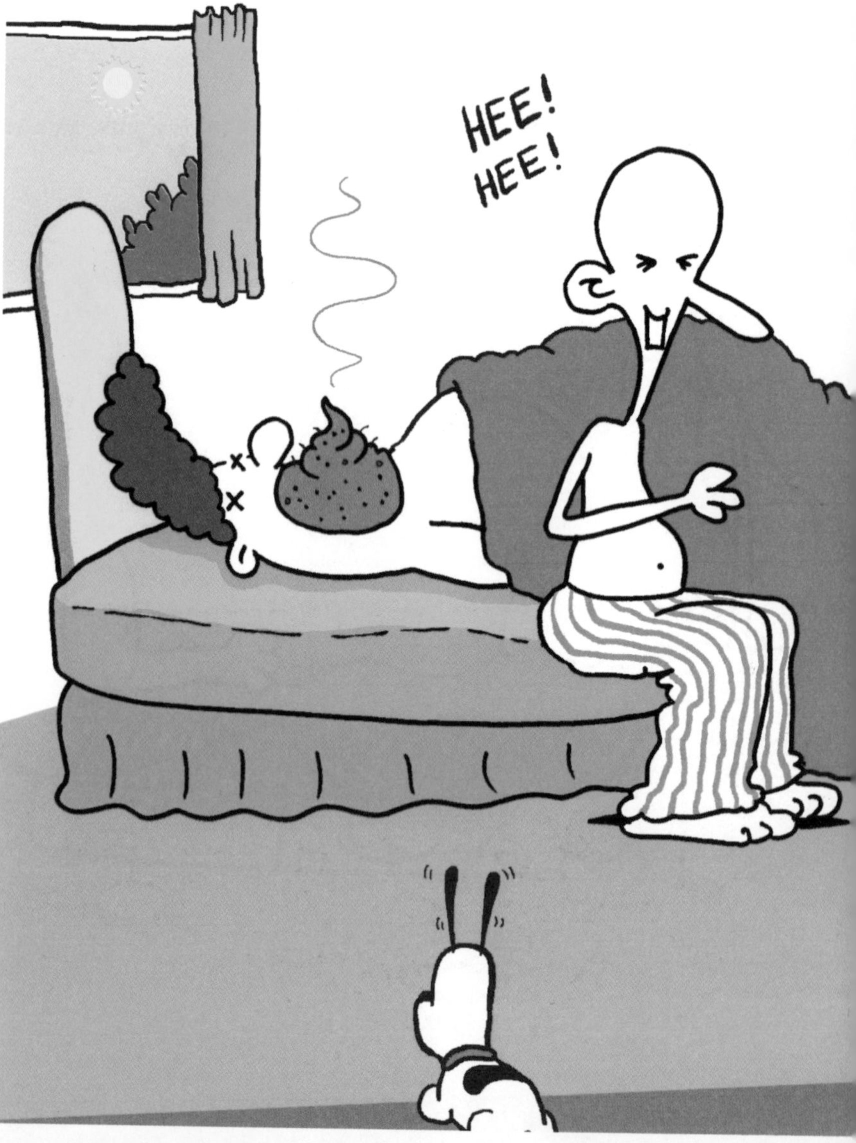
HEE! HEE!

STRANGE. ALTHOUGH JEFF WAS SURE THE TIPPEX WAS EMPTY, NOW IT WAS FULL TO THE BRIM

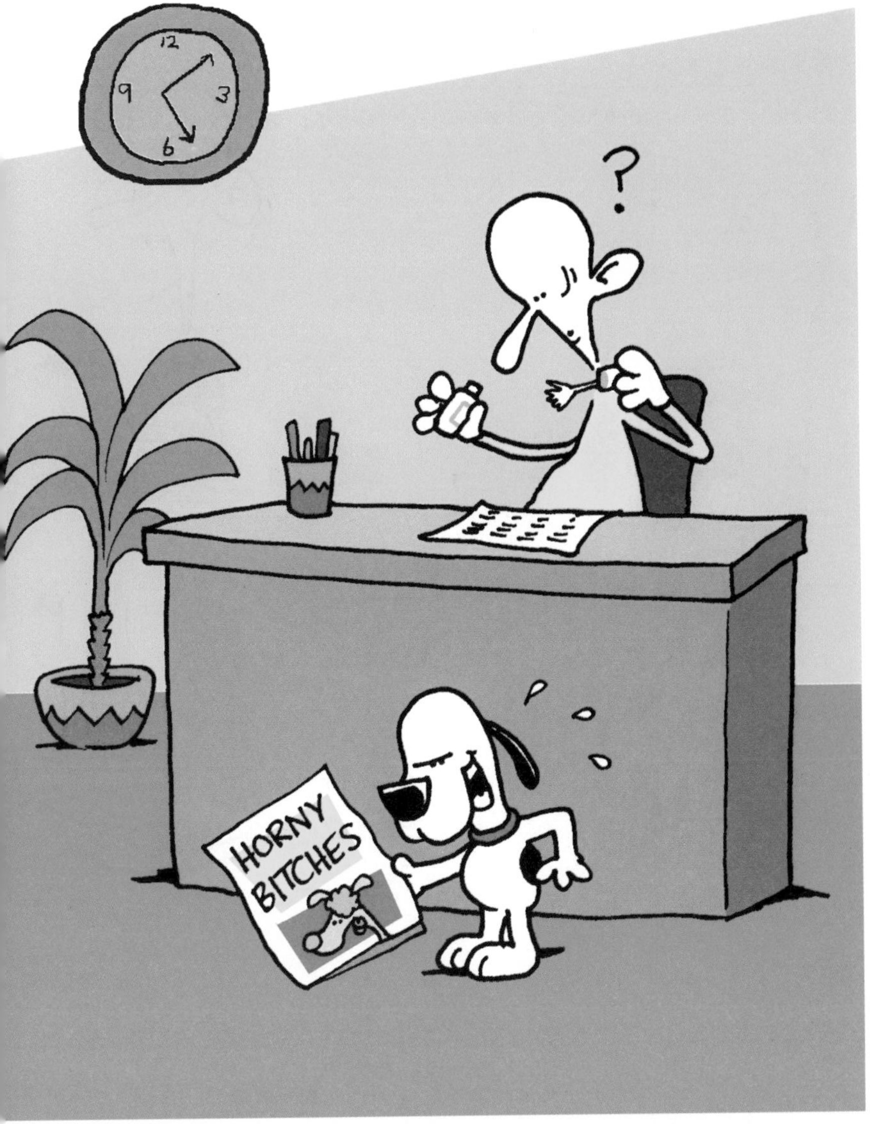
HORNY BITCHES

AFTER TRYING FOR SEVERAL PAINFUL HOURS TO PULL OUT A TINY POO STUCK TO HIS BUM HAIRS, JEFF DECIDED JUST TO LEAVE IT

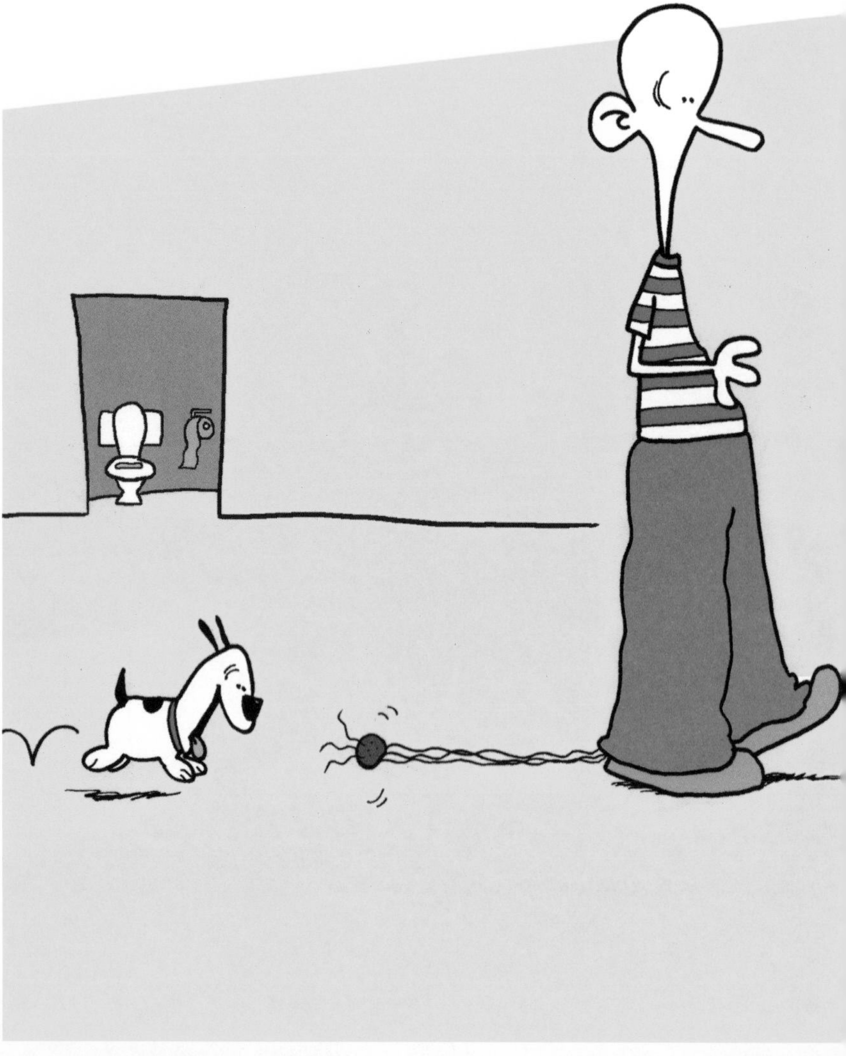

TO HER HORROR, MAUDE DISCOVERS WHAT HER FRIEND DOES WHEN SHE RUNS OUT OF MILK

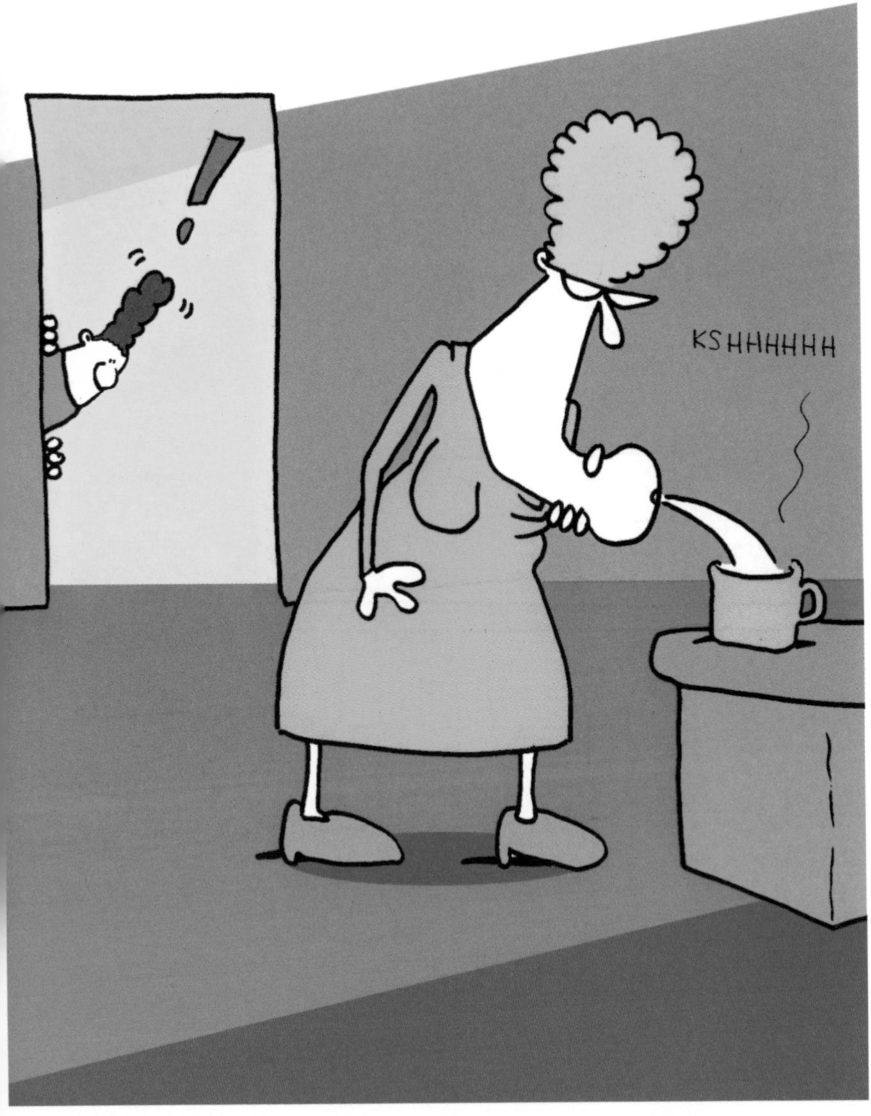
KSHHHHHH

FUNNY, THOUGHT LILY, SHE DIDN'T REMEMBER THE DOUGHNUT SHE BOUGHT HAVING A CUSTARD TOPPING

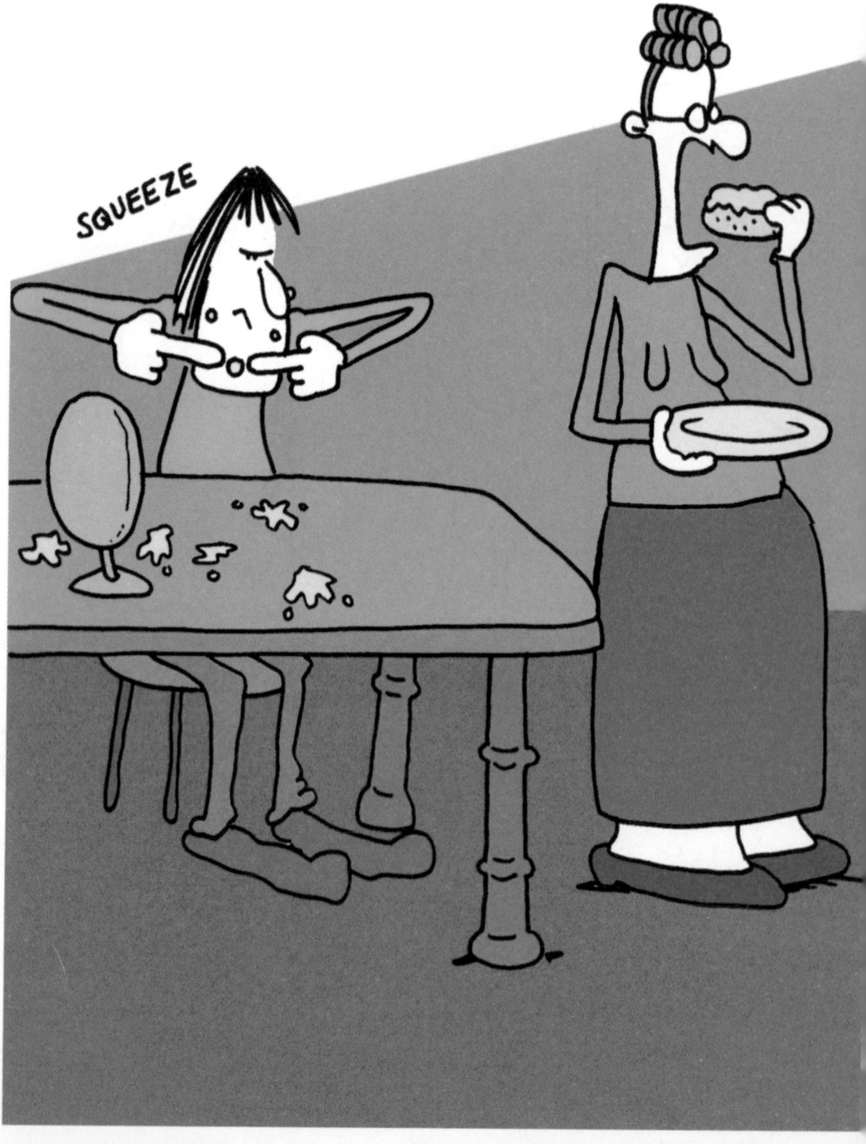
SQUEEZE

JEFF HAD PICKED HIS NOSE
A BIT TOO DEEPLY THAT TIME

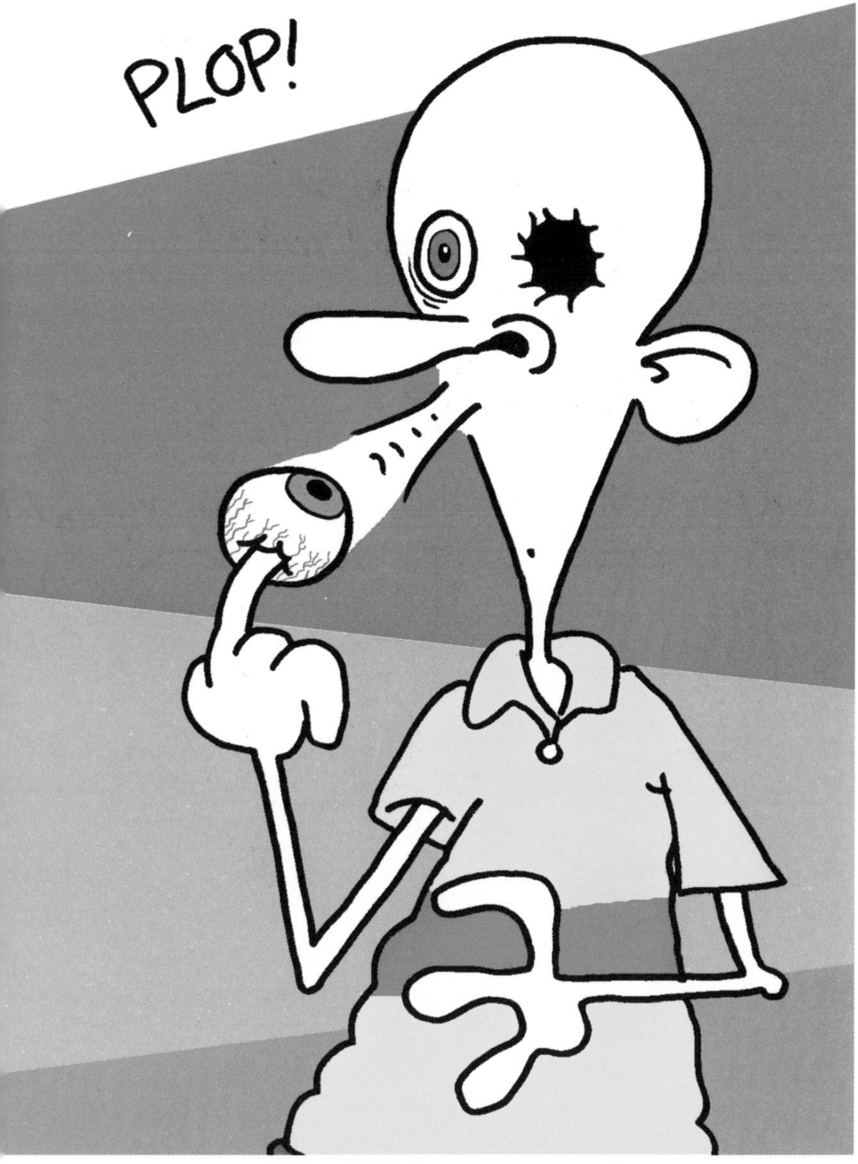
PLOP!

WHEN EATING IN RESTAURANTS, BEWARE OF ORDERING MEALS WHICH CONTAIN 'CHICK PEA'

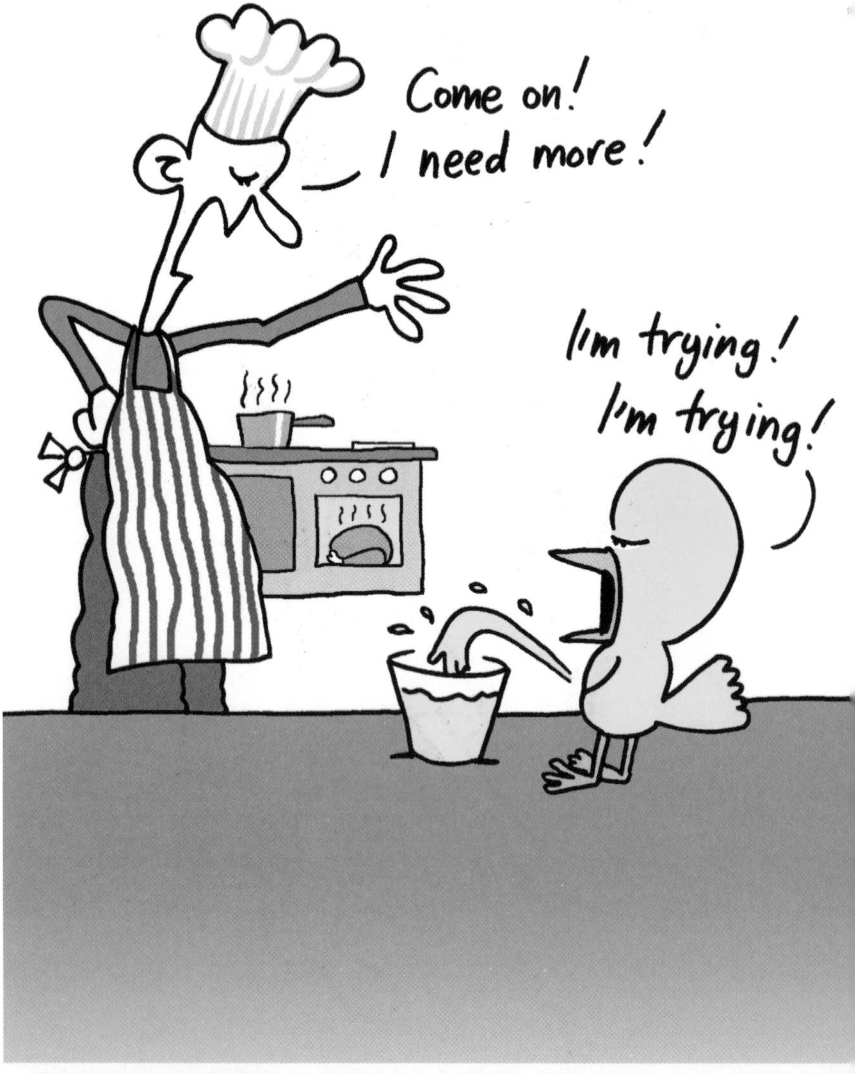
Come on! I need more!
I'm trying! I'm trying!

DUG DISCOVERS THAT IF YOU GO TOO DEEP DURING ORAL SEX THE GAG REFLEX CAN OCCUR

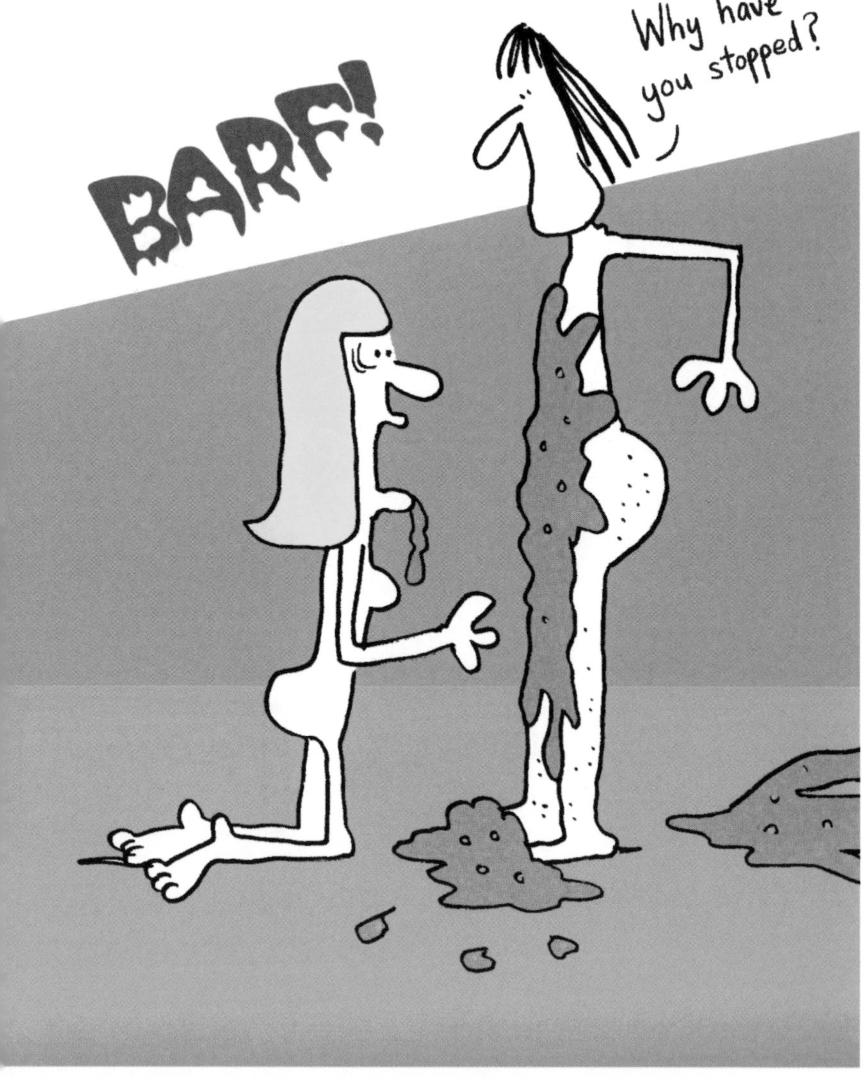
BARF!
Why have you stopped?

ONLY WHEN BLOWING UP HIS NEW SEX DOLL DID JEFF REALISE HE'D BEEN GIVEN THE WRONG MODEL

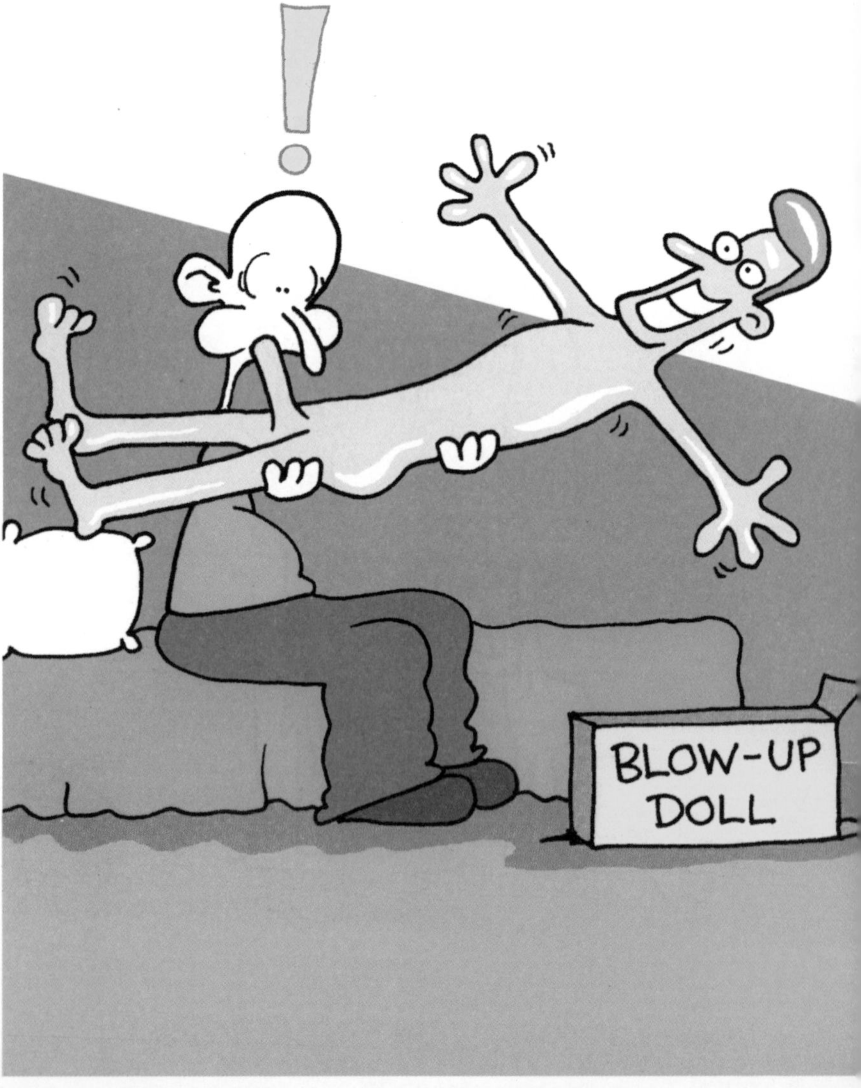
BLOW-UP DOLL

MAUDE CLEVERLY TURNS HER DODGY BOUT OF DIARRHOEA INTO A SUCCESSFUL BUSINESS

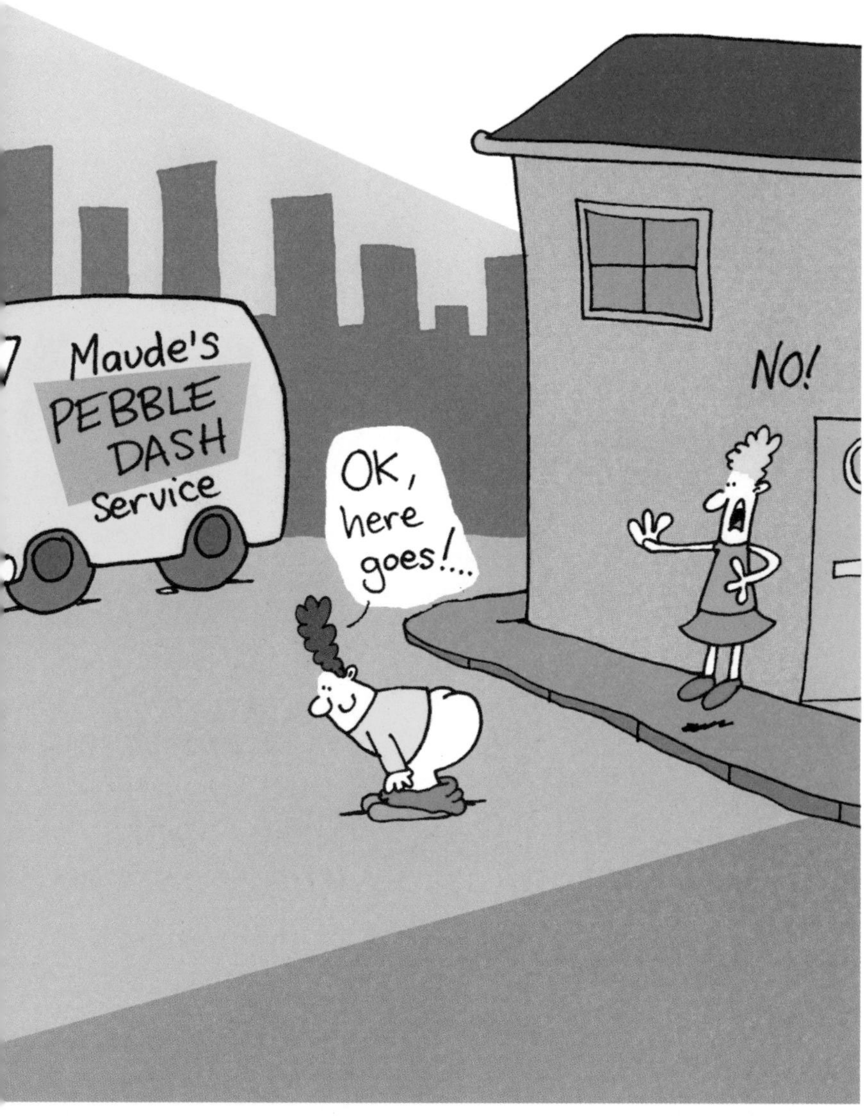
Maude's
PEBBLE DASH
Service
OK, here goes!...
NO!

JEFF LOVED LETTING THE DOG SLEEP ON THE BED BECAUSE OF THE LOVELY WARM FEELING HE GOT THROUGH THE BED

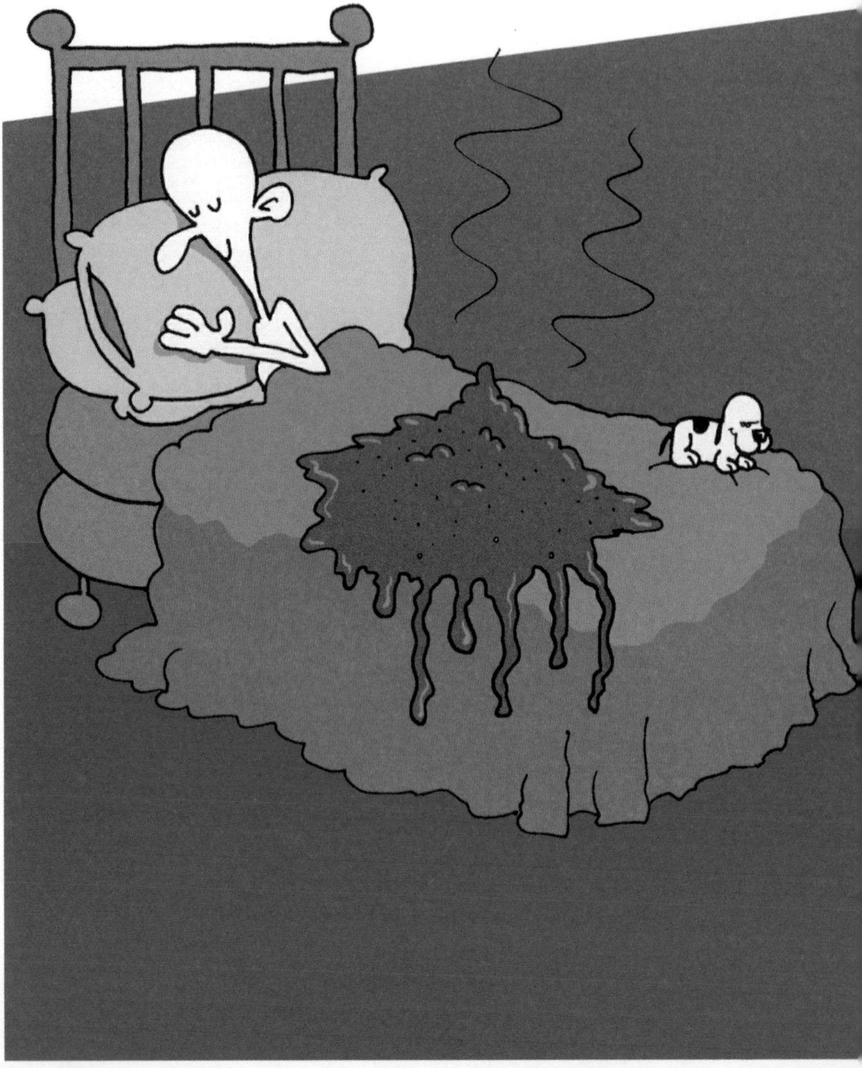

UNFORTUNATELY, DUG'S CLAIM THAT HE HAD A "WILLY LIKE THE HULK" WAS ONLY HALF TRUE

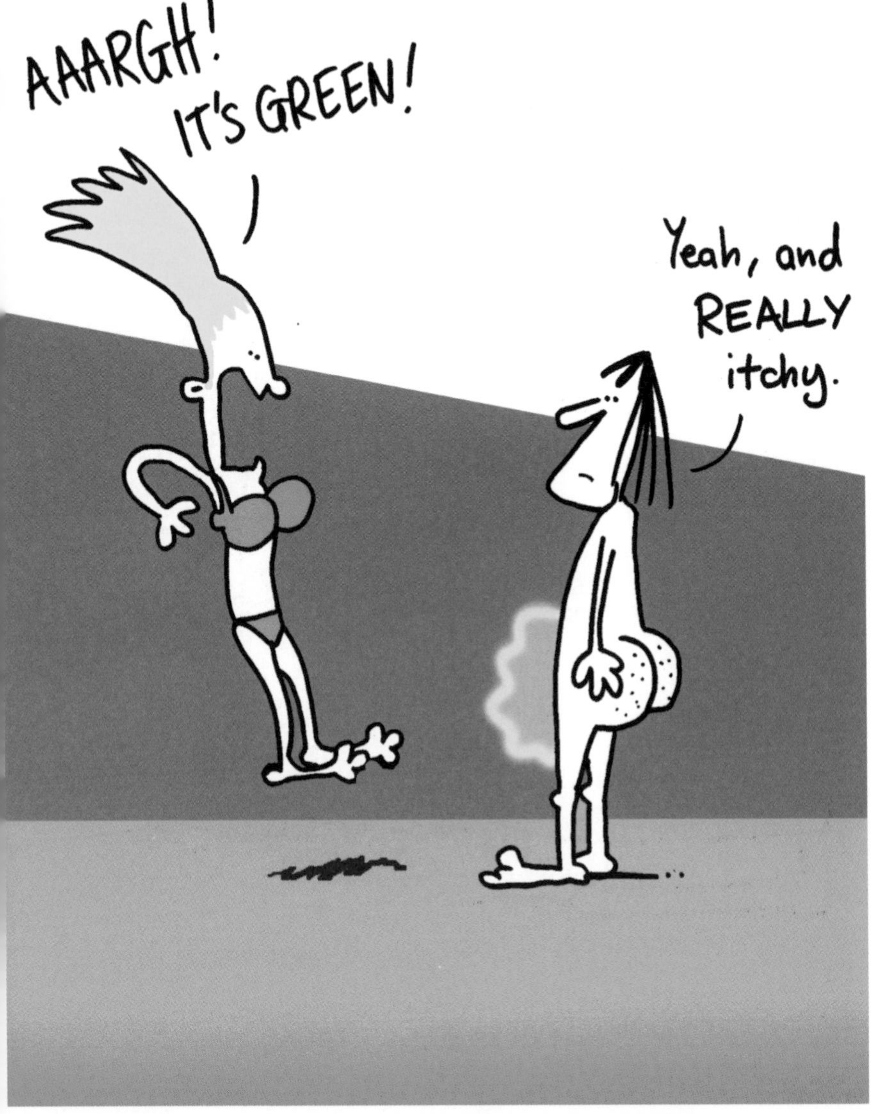
AAARGH! IT'S GREEN!
Yeah, and REALLY itchy.

MAUDE HAD A FUNNY FEELING
JEFF HAD BEEN LOOKING
AT INTERNET PORN AGAIN

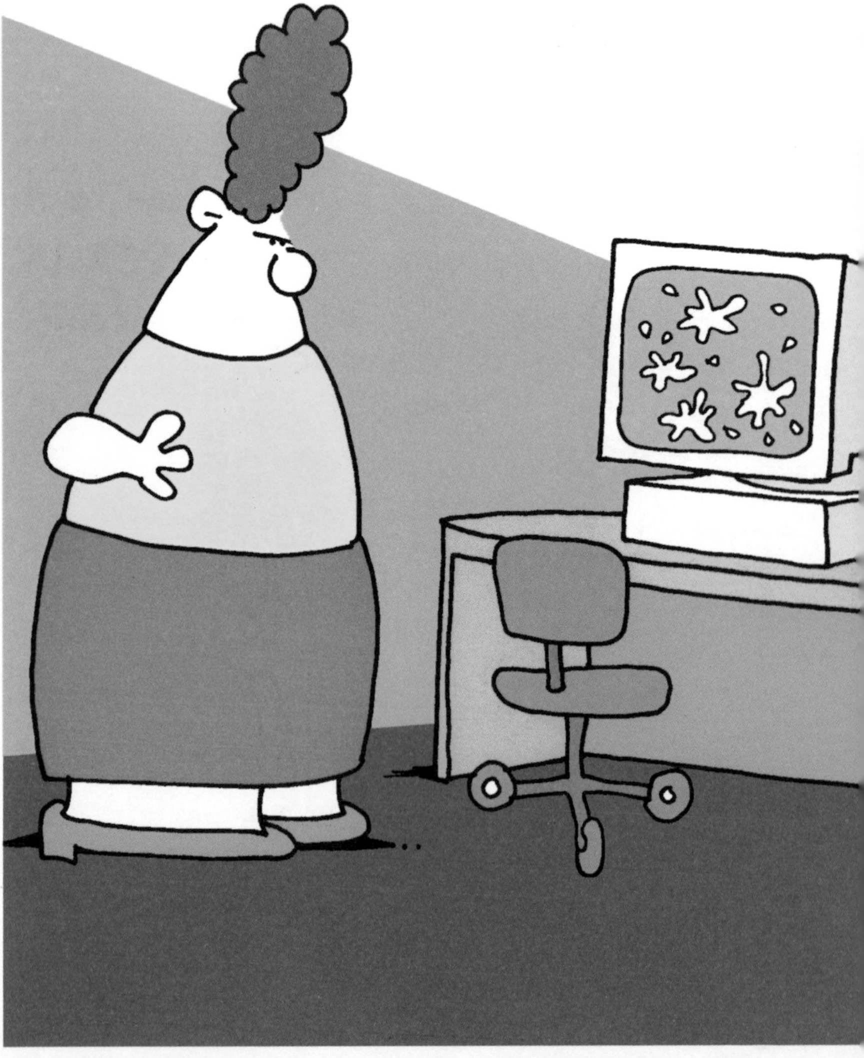

AFTER HER MAMMOTH SEX SESSION
MAUDE HAD A FEELING
SHE WAS STILL DRIBBLING

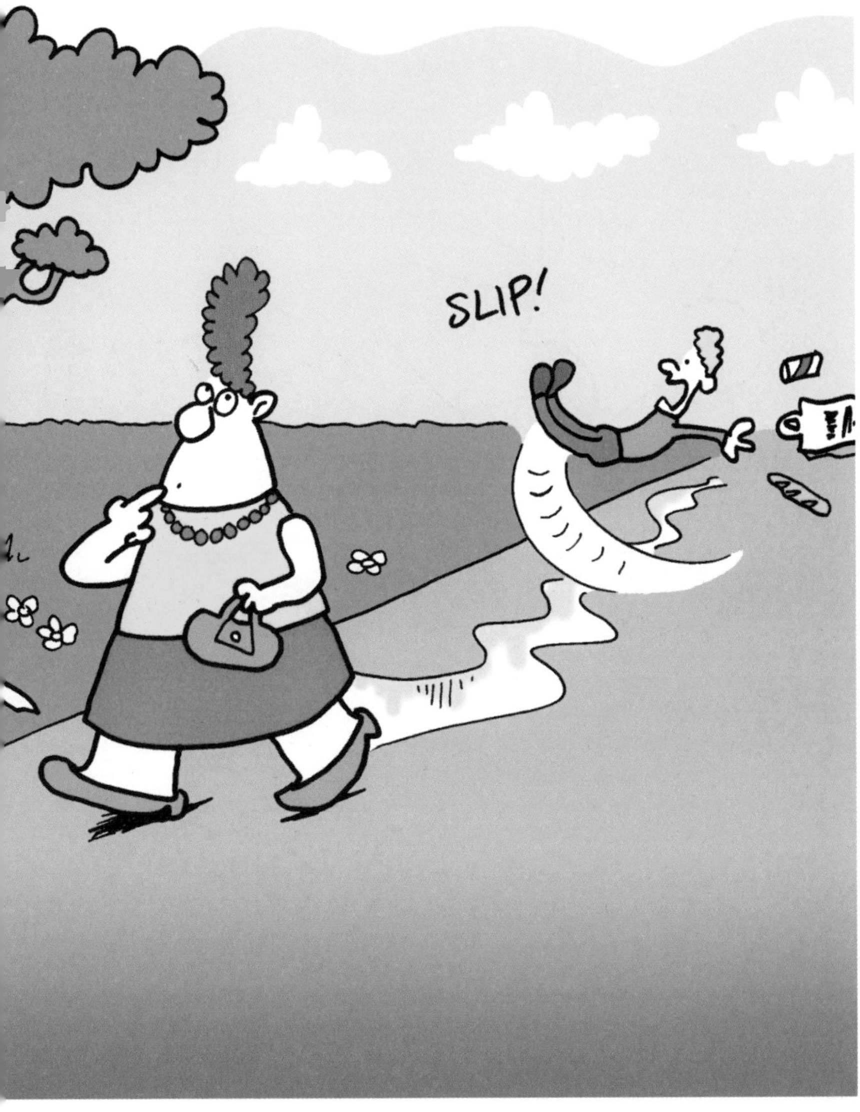
SLIP!

THE LAST TIME JEFF EVER DRANK IN A PUB GARDEN: THE DAY HE NEGLECTED TO NOTICE THE BIRD POO IN HIS PINT

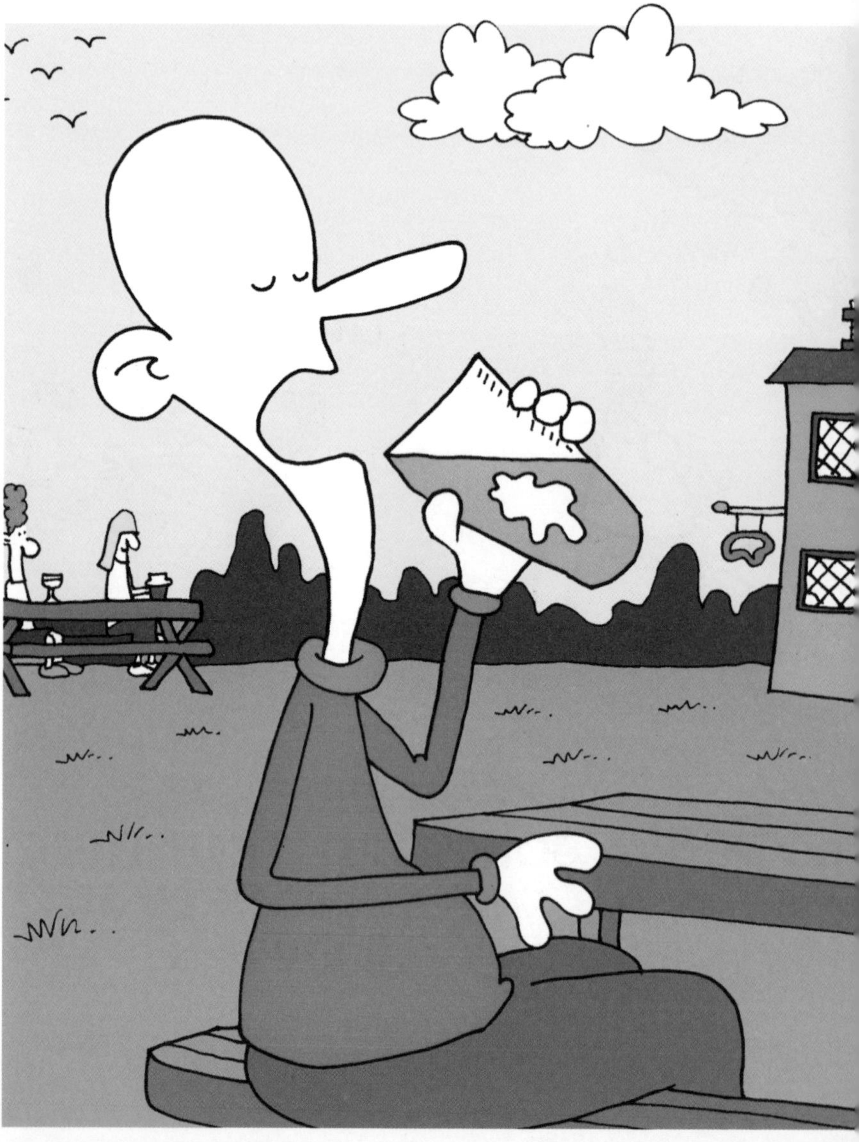

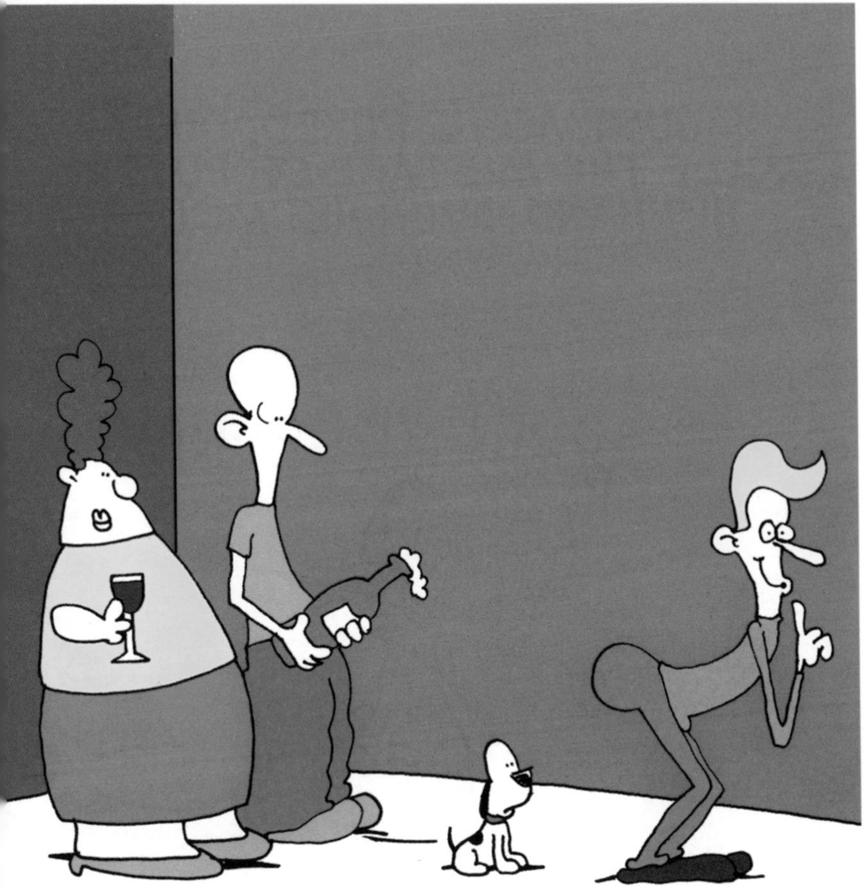

NO-ONE KNEW WHERE THE CORK HAD GONE. BUT THEN THEY NOTICED CAMP COLIN SEEMED SUDDENLY CHEERFUL...

JUST AS HE PUKED, DUG MADE THE MISTAKE OF PUTTING HIS HAND OVER HIS MOUTH

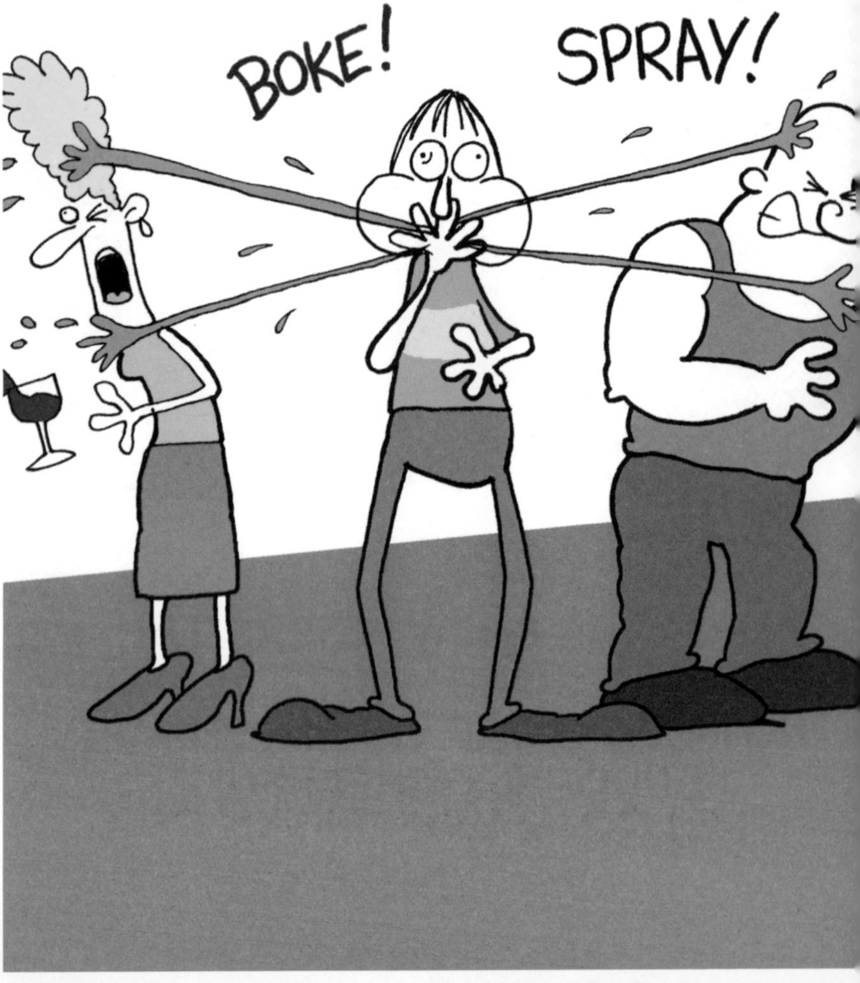
BOKE!
SPRAY!

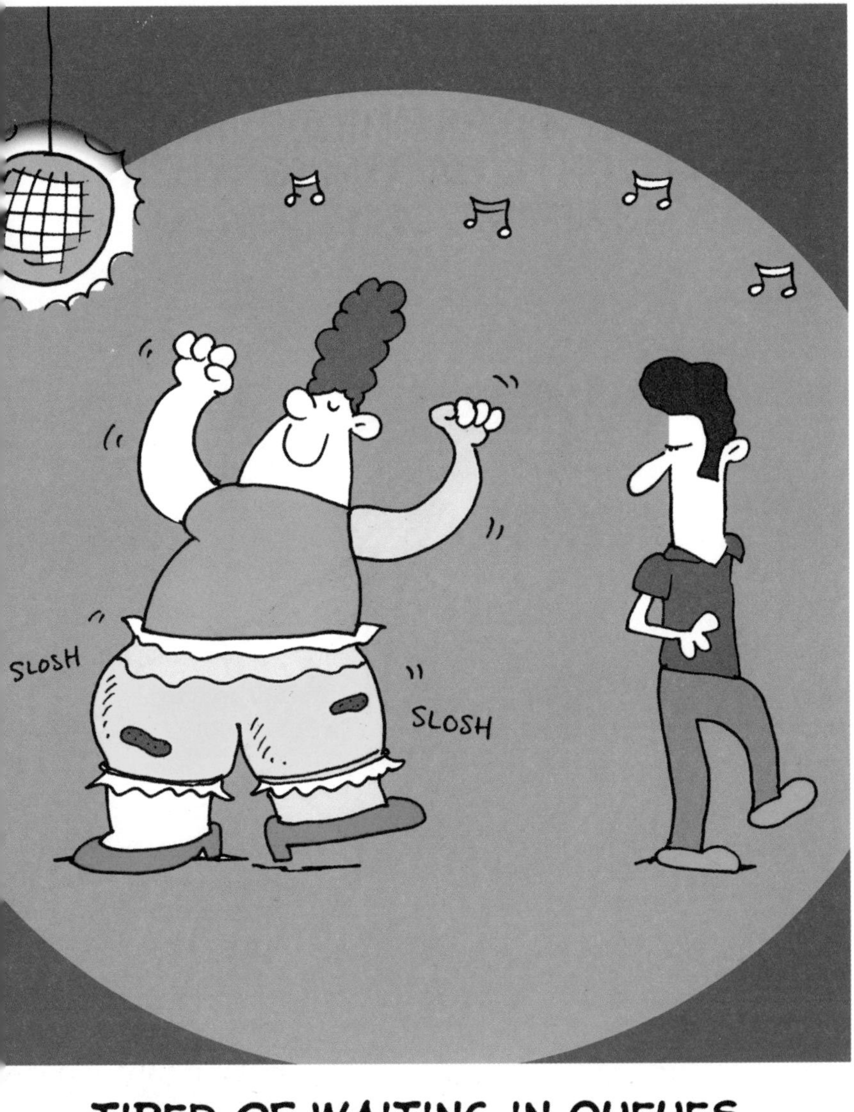
SLOSH
SLOSH

TIRED OF WAITING IN QUEUES IN NIGHT CLUBS TO GO TO THE LOO, MAUDE THINKS OF A BETTER PLAN

TO CLEAR UP MESSY PILES OF SICK AT PARTIES, SIMPLY WAIT UNTIL MORNING WHEN THEY'VE DRIED UP

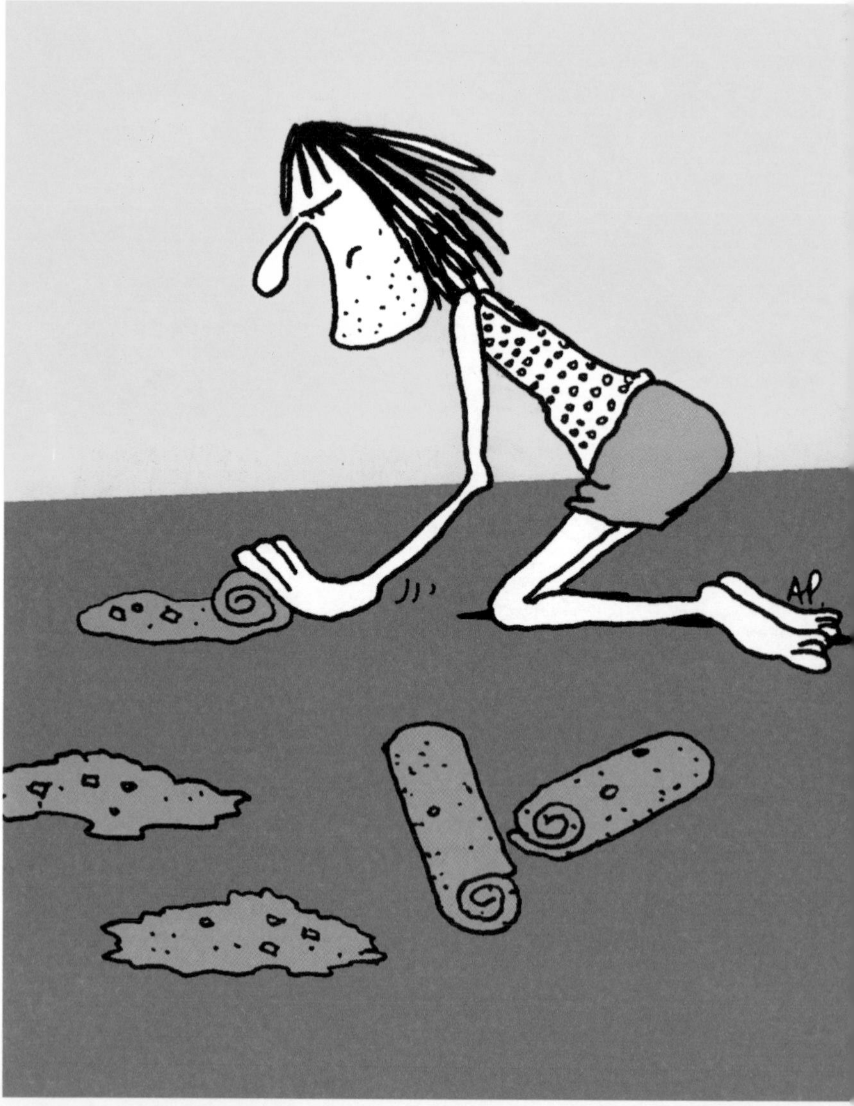
AP.

TIRED OF PICKING UP THE DOG'S POOS, JEFF THINKS OF A BETTER IDEA

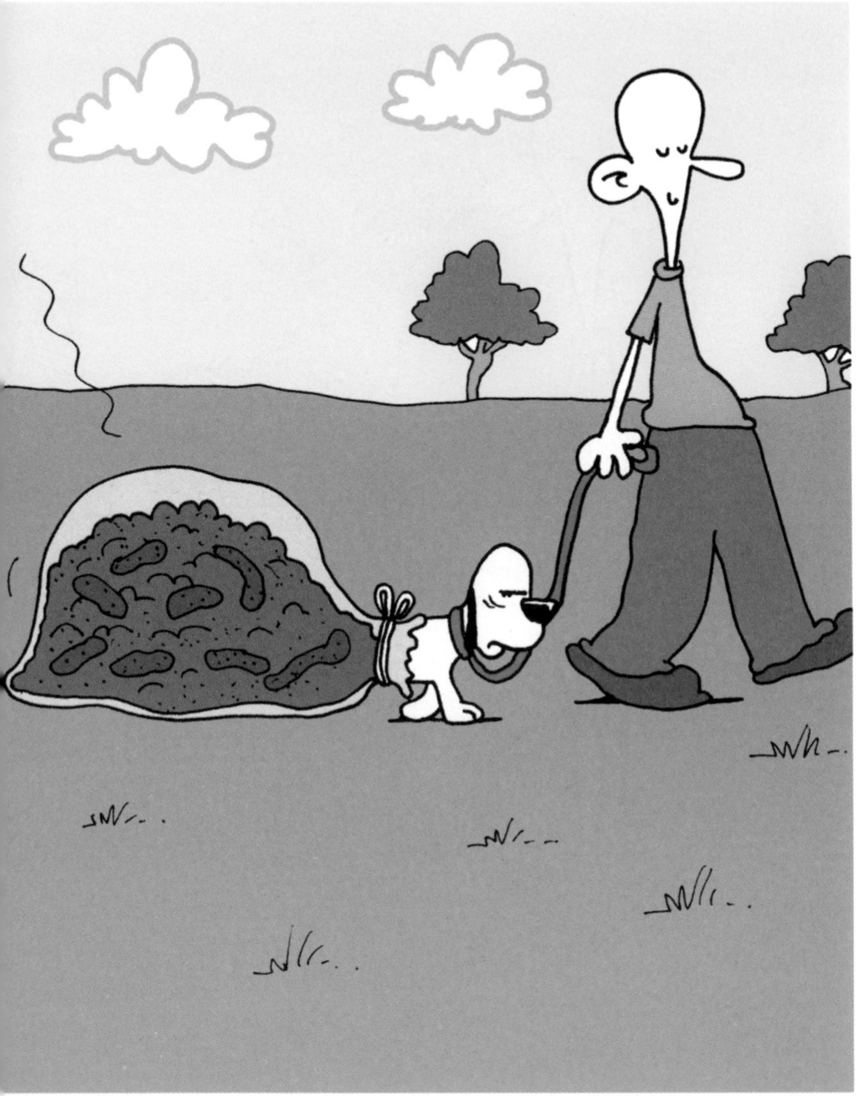

JEFF WENT TO THE DOCTOR TO HAVE A WORRYING MOLE REMOVED

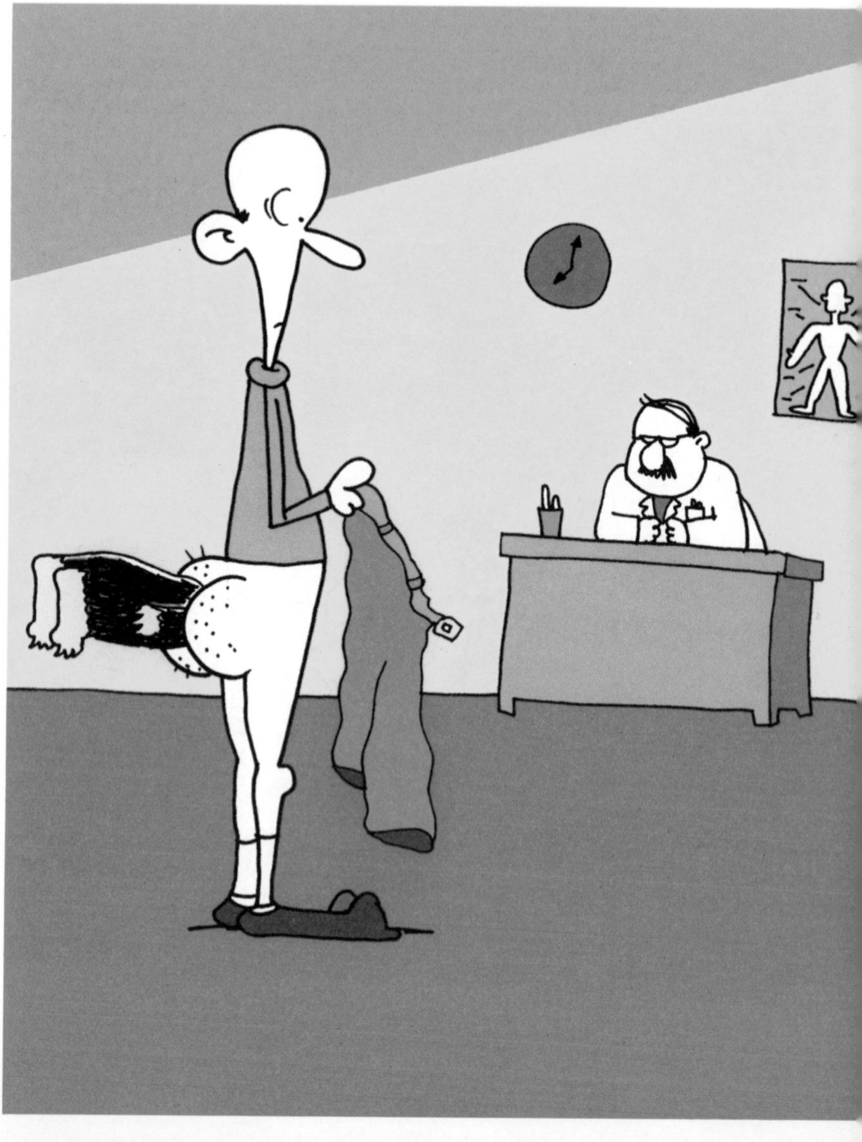

MAUDE'S DATE LOOKED VERY DIFFERENT IN THE MORNING AND HIS BREATH SMELLED TERRIBLE!

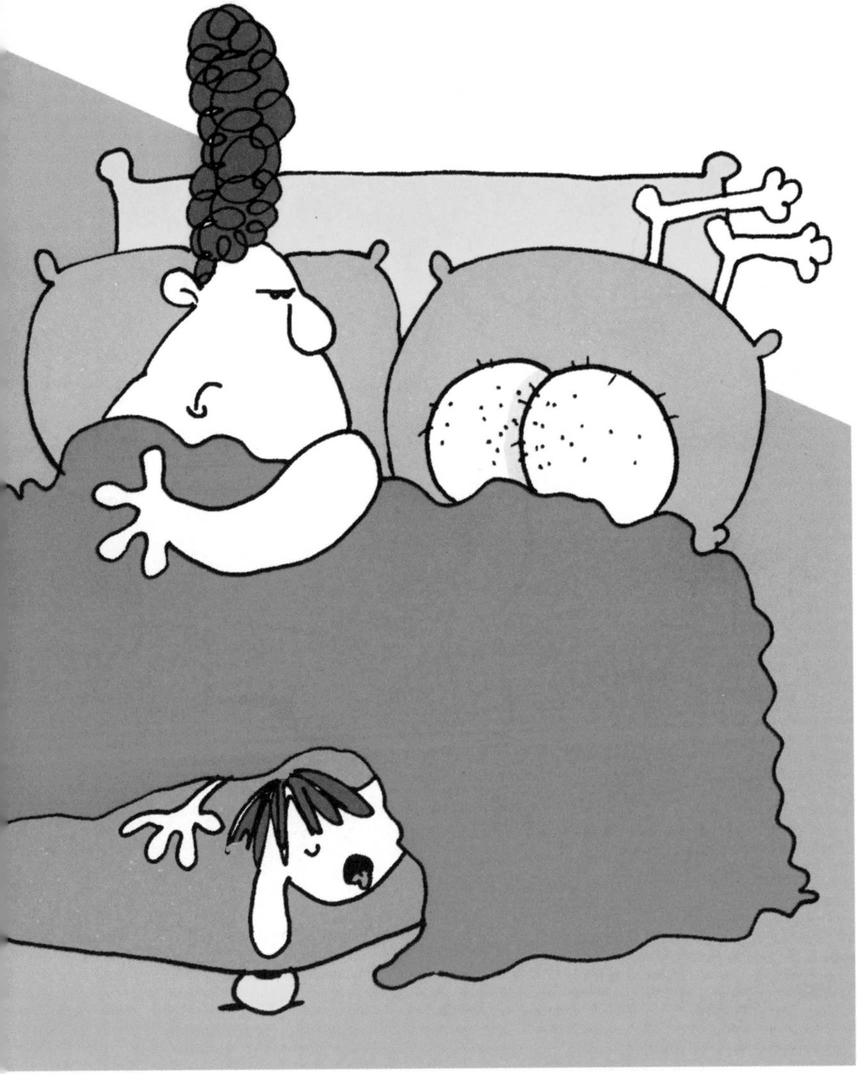

JEFF'S DOG DISCOVERS THAT TRUDIE WAS NOT IN FACT A TRUE BLONDE

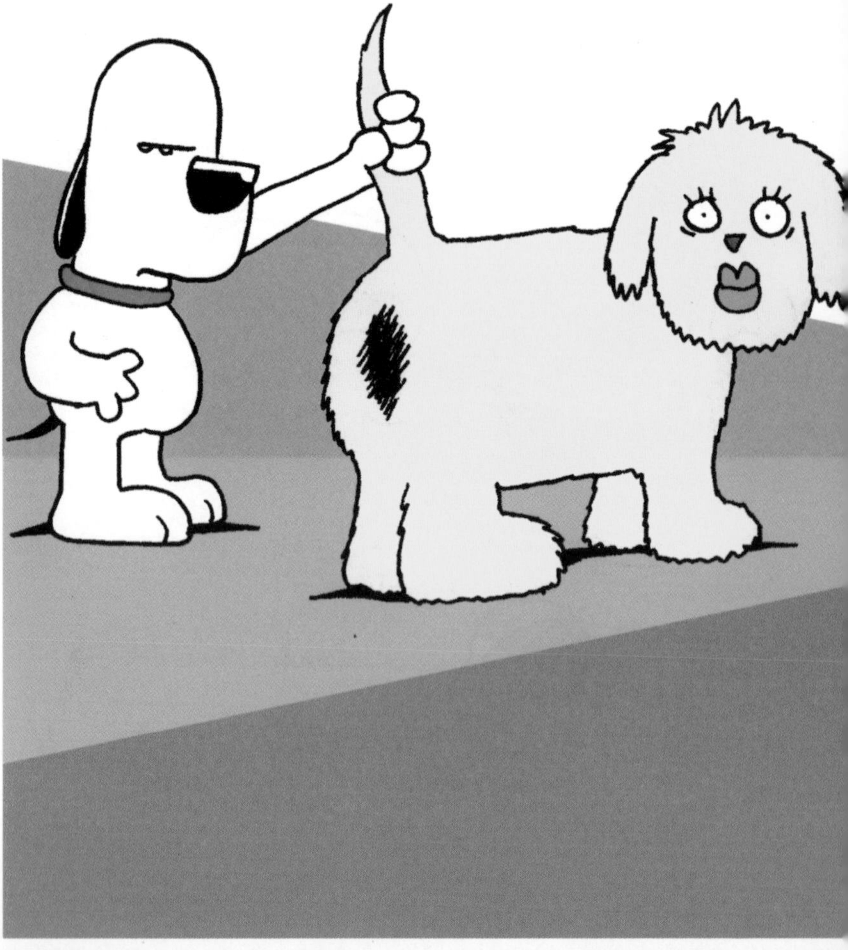

KEEN TO HELP THE BIRDS DURING WINTER, LILY LEAVES THEM OUT A LITTLE SNACK

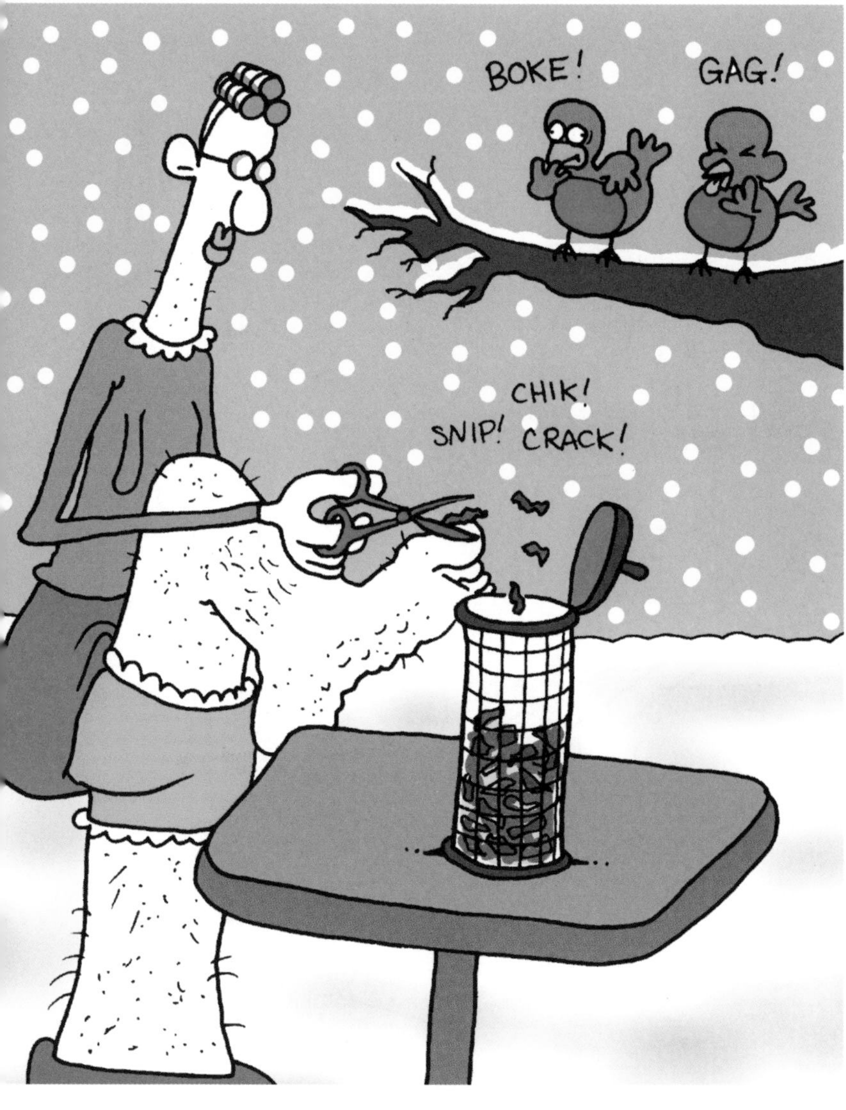
BOKE!
GAG!
CHIK!
SNIP!
CRACK!

FED UP WITH TRYING TO UNDO SARAH'S BRA, DUG TAKES DRASTIC ACTION

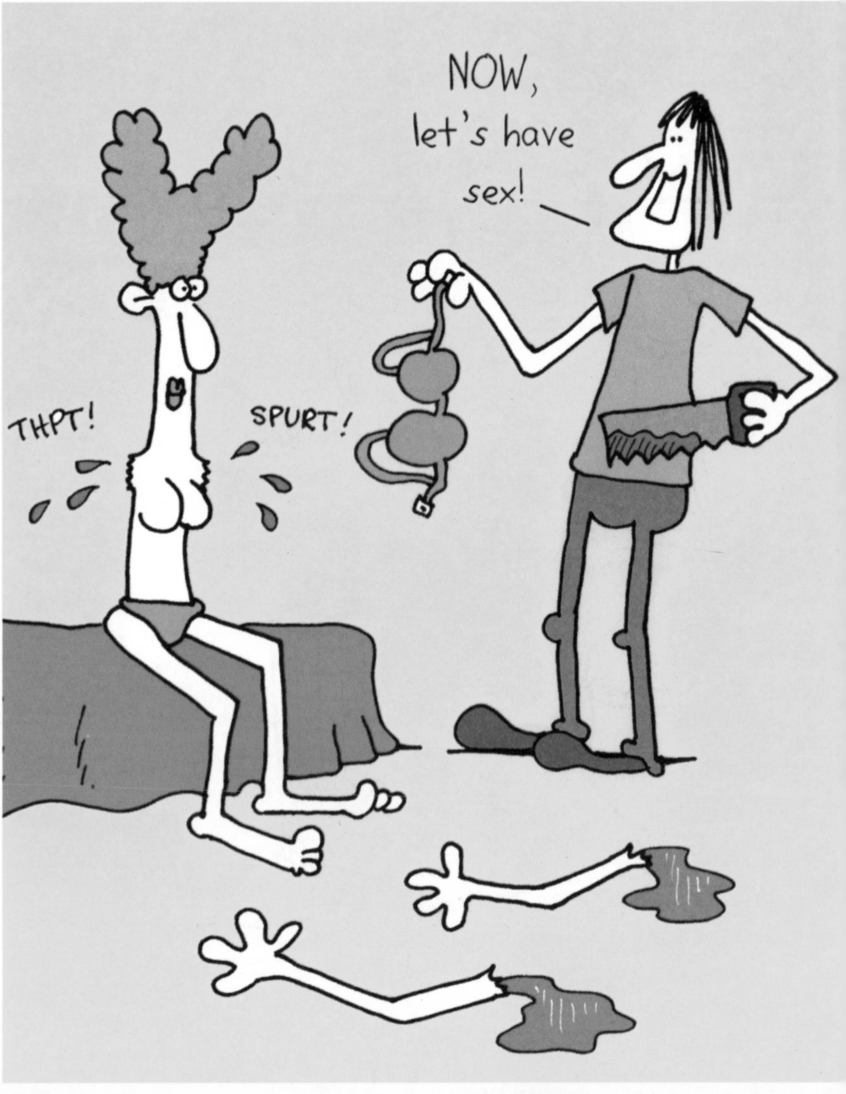
NOW, let's have sex!
THPT!
SPURT!

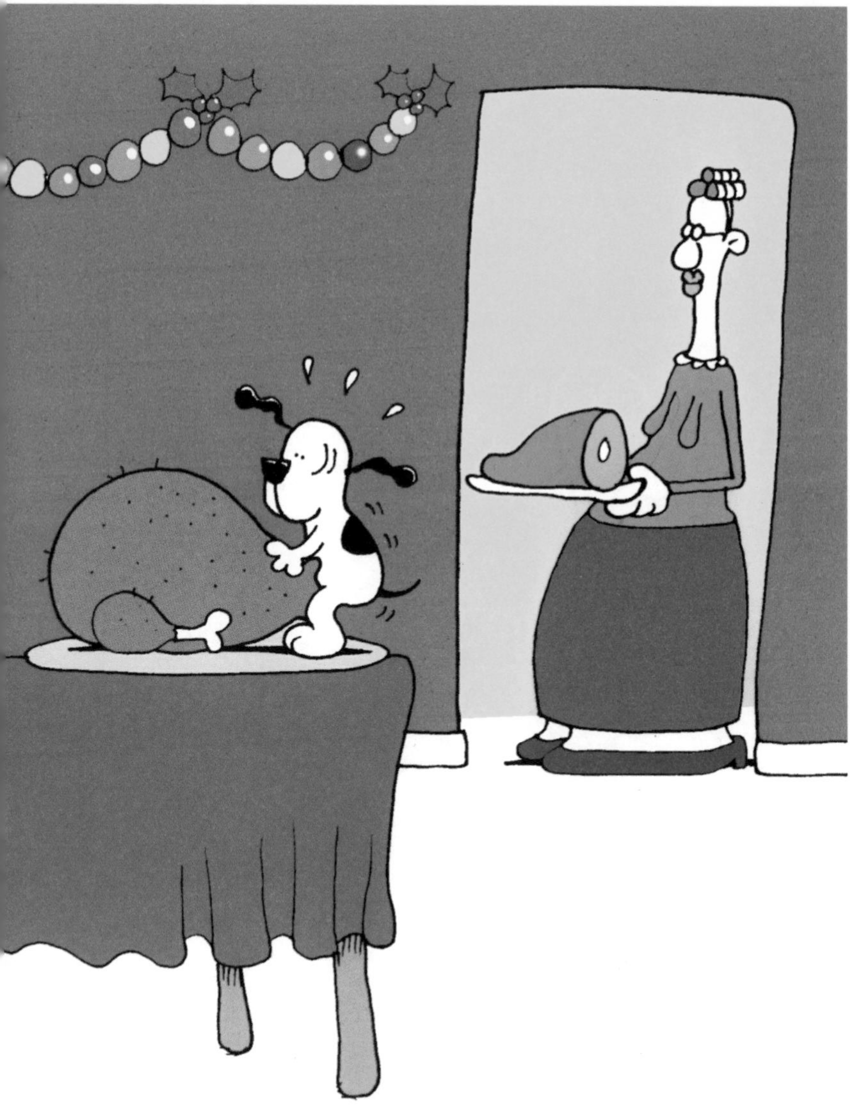

AFTER DISCOVERING THE DOG
WITH THE TURKEY, LILY
DECIDED TO SERVE THE HAM

JEFF DISCOVERED THE BENEFITS OF A POO THAT WOULDN'T BREAK OFF

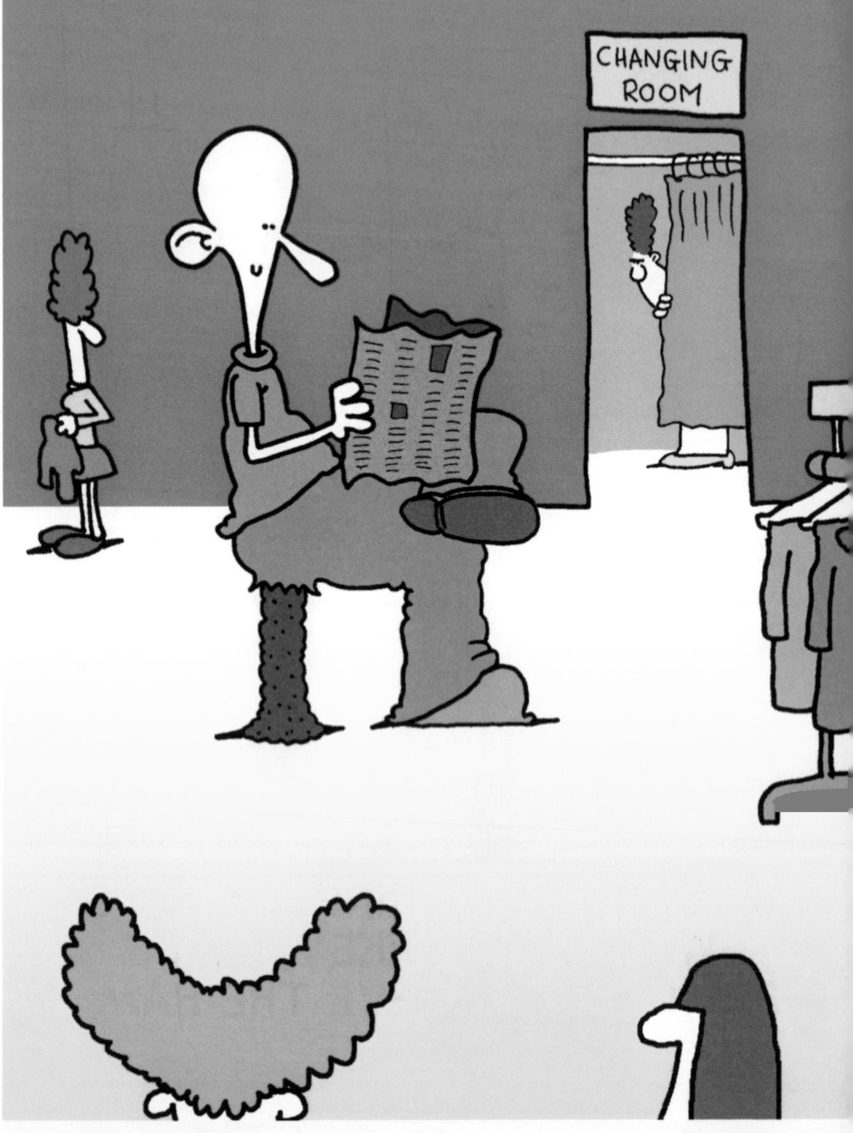
CHANGING ROOM

MAUDE COULDN'T BELIEVE JEFF – FIRST HE MAKES HER A NICE MEAL AND NOW THIS!

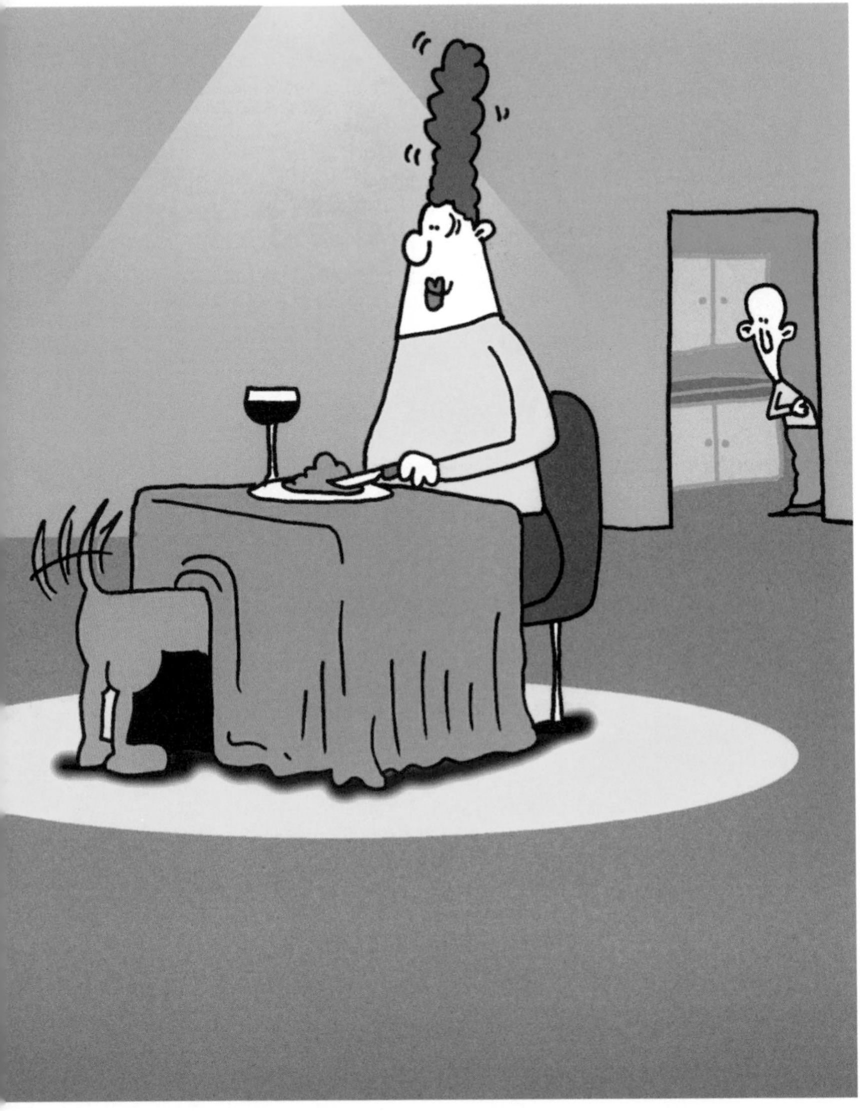